The TRUMAN YEARS

The Words and Times of
Harry S. Truman

This political button, measuring nine inches in diameter,
was made for President Truman's 1948 Presidential campaign.

Independence and the Opening of the West
— Truman Library mural

The large mural, *Independence and the Opening of the West* by Thomas Hart Benton (1889-1975), a Missourian and friend of Truman, adorns the lobby wall in the Harry S. Truman Library in Independence, Missouri, Truman's home town. The painting depicts the strength of the hardy settlers and travelers heading west. Independence was the thriving gateway for wagon trains traveling over the Santa Fe and Oregon trails in the mid-nineteenth century. Truman's grandfather led wagon trains to California along the Oregon Trail, and in the 1920's Truman, who had a profound interest in American history, was president of the National Old Trails Association. In the lower right corner is the Jackson County Courthouse (see pages 10-11).

The TRUMAN YEARS
The Words and Times of
Harry S. Truman

By the Editors of COUNTRY BEAUTIFUL

Editorial Direction: Michael P. Dineen
Edited by Robert L. Polley
Art Direction: Buford Nixon

COUNTRY BEAUTIFUL
Waukesha, Wisconsin

President Truman left his home in
Independence for a neighborhood walk, a favorite
pastime during his later years.

President Truman realized that the notion of isolationism,
of avoiding entangling alliances, no longer made sense in the postwar era.
His foreign policy was based on this realization.

COUNTRY BEAUTIFUL: *Publisher and Editorial Director:*
Michael P. Dineen; *Vice President, Editorial:* Robert L. Polley;
Vice President, Operations: Donna Griesemer; *Vice President,
Sales:* Wm. B. Chappie; *Managing Editor:* John M. Nuhn
(House Editor); *Art Director:* Buford Nixon; *Senior Editors:*
James H. Robb, Kenneth L. Schmitz, Stewart L. Udall;
Research: Ann Gohlke; *Associate Editor:* Kay Kundinger;
Editorial Assistant: Wendy Weirauch; *Art Assistant:* Ann Baer;
Marketing Director: Jeanie Holzwart; *Sales Manager:* Mary
Moran; *Production:* John Dineen; *Assistant to Publisher:* Gay
Ciesinski; *Administration:* Roy Adolph, Rita Brock, Karen
Ladewig, Dolores Wangert.

Country Beautiful Corporation is a wholly owned subsidiary of Flick-Reedy
Corporation; President: Frank Flick.

Library of Congress Cataloging in Publication Data

Truman, Harry S., Pres., U.S., 1884-1972.
    The Truman years.

    1. United States—Politics and government—1945-
1953—Collected works. 2. Truman, Harry S., Pres.
U.S., 1884-1972. I. Polley, Robert L. II. Country
beautiful. III. Title.
E742.5.T62   1976.   973.918′092′4 [B]   75-45336
ISBN 0-87294-083-7

PHOTO CREDITS: Authenticated News International, 48 bottom, 94,
108; Bagby Studio, South Bend, Indiana, 36 top; Black Star, 50-51 (both), 53,
60, 63, 66, 74, 83, 84, 88-91 (all), 96-100 (all), 103-105 (all), 112; Marvin
Koner from Black Star, 54-55, 57, 58-59; John Launois from Black Star, 4, 6;
Roland Patterson from Black Star, 107; Caufield and Shook, Louisville, 34
bottom; Dellenbach from the University of Indiana, 25 top right; Field
Enterprises (*Chicago Sun-Times*) from the Truman Library, 56 left (by George
Sixta), 87; Embassy of Israel, 42 top; Harris and Ewing from the Truman
Library, 47; Jackson County Historical Society, 10-11; *Kansas City Journal*
from the Truman Library, 15 bottom; *Kansas City Star*, from the Truman
Library, 7, 9, 15 top; Keystone Press Agency, 22 bottom right, 31 top, 34 top
left, 35, 39 (both), 40 top, 41 center and bottom, 43, 48 top, 49 bottom, 62,
85, 95, 96; National Basketball Association, 32 bottom left; National Park
Service from the Truman Library, 68; *National CIO News* from the
Truman Library, 69; Newspaper Enterprise Association from the Truman
Library, 77; Penguin Photos, 17-21 (all), 22 top and bottom left, 23, 24
(both), 25 bottom, 26-30 (all), 37 (both), 38, 56 right, 67 (all), 101, 102;
Photographics, courtesy of Don L. Taylor, 1; Truman Library, 2-3, 8-9, 12,
14, 46, 49 top, 76, 106, 111; U.S. Air Force, 41 top; U.S. Army, 79, 81, 86; U.S.
Army from the Truman Library, 78; U.S. Navy from the Truman Library,
44-45; United Press International, 25 top left, 31 bottom, 32 top, 33 (both),
34 top right, 36 right, 40 bottom, 42 bottom left and bottom right, 64, 70,
76, 80, 82, 92, 93, 109; UPI from the Truman Library, 61, 75; University of
Kentucky, 32 bottom right; University of Michigan, 36 center left;
Washington Post from the Truman Library, 65; White House Historical
Association, 16; Wide World Photos from the Truman Library, 72; Wide
World Photos from United Mine Workers, 52.

Truman was 13 in Independence when this photo was taken. He was warned not to play sports lest he break his glasses and risk serious eye injury. But he enjoyed reading, and by the time he graduated from high school he had read nearly every book in the Independence Public Library.

CONTENTS

Prologue 10

Kaleidoscope 1945-1952 17

1945: The Decision 44

1946: A Nation Divided 52

1947: The Cold War 58

1948: Giving 'Em Hell 64

1949: A Pact to Prevent War 72

1950: Land War in Asia 78

1951: Swings of the Pendulum 86

1952: McCarthyism and the Specter of
Communists in Government 92

Courage and Humility 100

Epilogue 104

Chronology 110

Truman's White House Oval Office *(left)* has been duplicated
in the Truman Library. The decorative items in the room and the large
chair are originals from the White House office. The famous sign on
his desk, "The Buck Stops Here," is backed by the phrase, "I'm from
Missouri." The two large portraits behind his desk are of his mother,
Martha Ellen, and his daughter, Margaret. Below the Franklin D. Roosevelt portrait on the left wall is a lithograph entitled, "Burning of
the U.S.S. Frigate *Missouri*, August 26, 1843." On the other side of
the room is a 1690 map of America and Truman's certification of
election, November 7, 1922, as judge of Jackson County — his first
certificate for holding public office. Lying-in-state ceremonies
for President Truman took place at the Truman Library *(above)* on
December 27, 1972. Margaret Truman Daniel, husband Clifton and
Truman's four grandchildren are to the left. He is
buried in the courtyard of the Truman Library.

Prologue

"Boys, if you ever pray, pray for me now," the new President said in his first meeting with reporters. ". . . When they told me yesterday what had happened, I felt as though the moon, stars and all the planets had fallen upon me."

When Harry S. Truman was sworn in as the thirty-third President of the United States on April 12, 1945, a few hours after Franklin D. Roosevelt had died, the nation was in the midst of its most traumatic days, as far as the Presidency was concerned, during the ninety-eight years between the assassinations of Lincoln and John Kennedy. Roosevelt had been President for twelve years, longer than anyone else, before or since. He was immensely endowed with charm, eloquence, fearlessness and a political astuteness and style raised to the level of brilliance. As he led the nation successfully through the Great Depression and World War II, a sizable majority of Americans came to worship him, as a smaller but no less dedicated number despised him. But not one ignored him or underrated him.

As the new President completed his oath in the Cabinet Room of the White House in his flat Missouri twang, the nation scarcely could believe that F.D.R. was no longer our President and it was even more difficult to accept the fact that this plain-looking, relatively little-known politician was to replace him. About the only facts well known about him were that he had been a product of the notorious political machine of Boss Tom Pendergast of Kansas City and that Truman had headed a busy and effective wartime Senate committee which investigated the nation's defense program.

After the shock of F.D.R.'s death had worn off, many Americans became uncertain of the future with the new President at the helm. Cabell Phillips of the *New York Times* recalls that when a group of the White House press corps was told of Roosevelt's death one of them said, with alarm: "Good God, Truman will be President." The citizenry — still striving to bring World War II to a victorious conclusion — would have been frightened if they had

been aware (as the new President was painfully aware) how little effort Roosevelt had made to keep his Vice President posted on the ongoing activities of the nation's government and the secrets of war.

In the minds of Americans outside Missouri Truman was a cardboard figure, a feisty campaigner, with a talent for political infighting, but with little apparent understanding of the broad issues at home or abroad. Although a Gallup Poll three months after he took office revealed that eighty-seven percent of the people supported him, that was more an indication of hope than confidence. Truman in fact appeared to be a most ordinary American whose only discernible positive qualities were honesty and a lack of pretense, which some commentators immediately mistook for a lack of dignity. After the masterful

aristocrat F.D.R., it was not easy to appreciate homelier virtues in a President.

But Harry S. Truman brought many more positive qualities to the Office of President than most of his countrymen saw. In addition to unpretentiousness and honesty, he brought the courage to make decisions, unpopular as well as popular ones. He had the stamina to see his tasks through to completion. And he had the ability to attract and lead men under stress, including men of great distinction, intelligence and achievement. Perhaps most surprising of all, Truman brought to his incumbency a comprehensive understanding of American history and of the essence of American democracy. In short, he brought both character and substance to the Presidency and he became a great President.

An old lithograph of Jackson Square in Independence illustrates that town's popularity to travelers embarking on trails west. The courthouse in the square was begun in 1829 to replace a log structure and has had five subsequent additions, with the existing building resembling Independence Hall in Philadelphia. Presiding Judge Truman began renovating and enlarging the courthouse in the 1920's. In 1934 he launched a statewide political campaign from these new offices that led to his election to the U.S. Senate. The original log courthouse has been preserved and is a historic site.

This painting of Truman's mother, Martha Ellen, was done
by Jerry Farnsworth in her latter years. "Mamma" Truman was a
liberal Baptist who combined fun, discipline and duties to provide
a healthy atmosphere for the young Harry. Coming from an upper middle
class family, she graduated from college with a major in music
and art, and thus encouraged Harry's efforts on the
piano and selected good books for him to read.

All of these qualities and abilities had been hewn from his sixty years of experience.* Born in a small white cottage in the village of Lamar, Missouri, Harry Truman's parents could never decide whether his middle name was that of his Grandfather Shippe or of his Grandfather Solomon, so only the "S" was used. Four years later his family moved to a farm in Jackson County and then, in 1890, to the county seat of Independence, where his father conducted a live-stock business. His mother, who was a strong in-fluence on him during her long life and a college graduate, taught Harry to read before he was five and to play the piano a little later. Harry began his school-ing in Independence when he was nine years old, but perhaps his most important education came outside the classroom. Afflicted from an early age with poor eyesight, he could not see well enough to play baseball and other sports so he spent much of his time in the Independence Public Library. By the time he was thirteen or fourteen he had read every book in the library. His favorite subject was history, which he continued to read for the remainder of his life. Repeatedly in later years he remarked upon the strong, positive influence his reading of history had on his Presidential decisions: "My debt to history is one which cannot be calculated."

His poor eyesight caused his rejection by the U.S. Military Academy at West Point, so after graduating from high school, he held a variety of jobs, including railroad timekeeper and bank clerk in Kansas City. In 1905 he joined the National Guard and a year later he returned to the family farm at Grandview in Jack-son County. Truman led a farmer's life until, in 1917, a few days after the United States declared war on Germany, he was sworn in as a first lieutenant of the Missouri National Guard. Participating in several battles of World War I in France, he was soon given command of Battery "D." His ability to lead his men who had a fearsome reputation as a "hardboiled bunch of Kansas City Irish," and to maintain discipline earned him much esteem. Thus the nagging sense of physical inadequacy he had carried over from child-hood was replaced by his new sense of command. "My whole political career is based upon my war service and war associates," he said many years later.

Shortly after returning from the war, he married "Bess" Wallace, whom he had admired since child-hood. He was thirty-five, a year older than she. After their honeymoon they settled down in the white clap-board house at 219 North Delaware Street in Inde-pendence, which remained their home for the rest of their lives, even while they lived in Washington, D.C.

In the fall of 1919, Truman formed a partnership with a regimental comrade, Eddie Jacobson, and opened a haberdashery shop in Kansas City. At first they did well, but the recession of 1921 hit their customers hard and the shop had to close the follow-ing year. Truman lost his entire life savings of

*For details and dates, see Chronology, pages 110-111.

$15,000 with added liabilities amounting to $20,000. But instead of filing for bankruptcy, he paid off his debts during the next fifteen years.

Harry Truman entered elective politics in 1922 (the same year his business failed) at the behest of Mike Pendergast, brother of Tom, the powerful Democratic political boss of Kansas City and en-virons. As a Baptist, a Mason, a war veteran and an ex-officer popular with his men, and with a reputa-tion for honesty, he was a successful candidate for Jackson County district judge, an administrative posi-tion which functioned like that of a county commis-sioner elsewhere. He suffered his only political defeat in 1924 when he ran for reelection, but in 1926 he was elected presiding judge of the county. During his eight-year tenure from 1927 to 1935, he furthered his reputation for honesty and added to it a penchant for efficiency and strict economy in spending $60 million of the taxpayers' money for highways and public buildings. When he ran for the Senate in 1934 at the age of fifty, Truman won with a plurality of 262,000 votes.

As a senator, he voted consistently for New Deal legislation, although his mentor, Tom Pendergast, was fervently anti-Roosevelt. Despite this and other demonstrations that he was his own man, Truman was sometimes called during his first term, "the Sen-ator from Pendergast," and he was unable to establish any rapport with the White House. He was an in-dustrious senator, but he seldom made a speech on the Senate floor. He was considered amiable but un-distinguished by the Senate hierarchy. He was also frustrated at trying to make ends meet for his family in Washington.

Truman was a despirited and financially strapped man as the elections of 1940 approached. Pendergast had been convicted of income tax evasion and had fallen from power. Some of Truman's best friends told him his chances of reelection were dim. He was thus confronted by a dilemma similar to that which he would face in 1948, and he came up with the same answer: He did not quit. He fought.

In a struggle for the Democratic nomination against the Missouri governor, Lloyd Stark, who was personally wealthy, Truman mounted a money-starved campaign. He bounced around the state in his old Chrysler coupe, sometimes driving alone, frequently spending twelve to fifteen hours a day in the swelter-ing summer sun visiting farms, villages and city halls. After receiving the benefits of last-minute support of the Democratic leader of St. Louis and a strong push for the incumbent by the railroad unions, Tru-man won renomination by the slender margin of 7,476 votes.

He won the election by a more comfortable margin and returned to Washington with increased respect from his colleagues. But it was his chairmanship of the Special Committee to Investigate the National

Captain Truman *(above, second row, fourth from left)* posed with officers of the 35th Division in France in 1919. Later that year he married Bess Wallace in Independence. Judge Truman relaxed at home with his wife and daughter *(opposite, top)* in 1934, the year he was elected to the U.S. Senate. Senator Truman left the Capitol in Washington *(opposite, bottom)* in June 1940. The following year he became chairman of the Truman Committee investigating the national defense program.

Defense Program prior to, as well as during, World War II that brought Senator Truman into the national limelight during his second term and set the stage for his selection by Roosevelt to be his running mate in 1944. After suggesting to the Senate the need for such a committee, Truman was chosen to head it and he put to good use his experiences as a county judge who had dealt with fly-by-night roadbuilders and contractors whose work was slipshod. Truman and his committee unearthed many examples of shoddy work, idle workers and costly bottlenecks due to bureaucratic red tape and exhorbitant profits in defense production. It was estimated that the exposure and correction of these abuses saved the taxpayers hundreds of millions of dollars.

Thus it was not too surprising that Senator Truman was considered a possibility for the Democratic Vice Presidential nomination in 1944. The incumbent, Henry A. Wallace, a moody and unpredictable liberal, was disliked and distrusted by many Democrats, particularly businessmen and Southerners. As the national nominating convention began in Chicago in July, another candidate much in the headlines was James F. Byrnes, former South Carolina Senator, former Supreme Court Justice, and now Director of War Mobilization (and later to be Truman's Secretary of State). Truman went to the convention com-

mitted to Byrnes, but President Roosevelt and the party leaders decided that the Senator from Missouri had the fewest handicaps and several strong points, such as his good standing with labor and his acceptability by the South, two factions in the party that could agree on little else.

Truman didn't consider himself a candidate and didn't want to be Vice President and when Robert Hannegan, Chairman of the Democratic National Committee (and the same St. Louis political leader whose support had been so important to Truman in the 1940 race for renomination), came to the senator's Chicago hotel room and told him that the President definitely wanted him on the ticket, Truman replied: "Tell him to go to hell." But he changed his mind and consented to having his name placed in nomination when Roosevelt said that if any one of the other contenders were nominated to run with him, the Democratic Party might well "break up." Wallace led Truman on the first ballot, but the senator easily won on the second one. With his running mate bearing the brunt of the campaign, Roosevelt easily won his fourth term as President in November. Five months later the man from Missouri became President.

Robert L. Polley

14

Pre-Presidential Years

I'll do my best and keep my feet on the ground. That's one of the hardest things for a senator to do, it seems. All this precedence and other hooey accorded a senator isn't very good for the republic.

The association with dressed-up diplomats has turned the head of more than one senator I can tell you. My trouble is that I probably won't find a place to live. You see, I have to live on my salary, and a cubbyhole rents for a hundred and fifty dollars a month there. The ones that are fit to live in run from two hundred and fifty to five hundred a month and although it's hard to believe, there are some saphead senators who pay fifteen hundred dollars a month for their apartments.

After Returning from First Visit to Washington, D.C.,
as Newly Elected Senator
November 1934

. . . To entrust the winning of the war and the framing of the peace to the hands of any man with a limited outlook and without the experience needed for such a job would be the sheerest folly. It might easily place the future of the nations and of the world in jeopardy. Let us show the nations of the world that America stands solidly united against her enemies. In the crucial days ahead let us continue on to final victory under the proven leadership of our commander-in-chief, Franklin Delano Roosevelt.

Campaign Speech as Vice Presidential Nominee
August 22, 1944

If a nation is to be run for profit first and people second, this fact of higher productivity means certain ruin, ruin for labor and ruin for business. But now reverse the order of importance, put human welfare first and profits second, and this same productivity which science has given us becomes the most wonderful phenomenon of our times.

Labor Day Speech to A.F.L. in Detroit
September 4, 1944

This portrait of President Truman, by Martha G. Kempton, hangs in the White House.

Kaleidoscope
1945-1952

Events and personalities — enduring and ephemeral — as World War II ends and the postwar world begins . . .

President Truman has a lighthearted conversation with child actress Margaret O'Brien, who seemed to symbolize the hope for a return to normal times during the postwar years. Margaret's first film, at age four, was *Babes on Broadway* (1941) with Judy Garland and Mickey Rooney. Among her other films were *Meet Me in St. Louis* (1944), *Our Vines Have Tender Grapes* (1945), *Tenth Avenue Angel* (1947) and *Little Women* (1949). Other young stars of the postwar years included Shirley Temple, now a teenager, and Peggy Ann Garner, probably most recognized for her starring role in *A Tree Grows in Brooklyn* (1945).

Hollywood newcomer Lauren Bacall joins Vice President Truman at the piano
(opposite, left) at the National Press Club in Washington, D.C., in early 1945,
a photo which became widely published. Bacall married Humphrey Bogart *(opposite, right)*
that same year after making her film debut with him in *To Have and Have Not* (1944). Her
other film credits include *The Big Sleep* (1946) and *Key Largo* (1948), also with Bogart.
One of Hollywood's greatest stars, Bogart appeared with Walter Huston and Tim Holt *(opposite,
bottom)* in the classic, *The Treasure of Sierra Madre* (1947). In 1951 he won an Academy Award for
The African Queen with co-star Katharine Hepburn. Gary Cooper won his second Academy Award
in 1952 for his performance as the determined lawman in *High Noon (below, right)*. His first
award had come in 1941 for *Sergeant York*; he also starred in *Task Force* (1949) and *You're
in the Navy Now* (1951). Rising starlet Elizabeth Taylor arrives for a Hollywood premiere
with her escort, football All-American Glenn Davis *(below, left)*, known as "Mr. Outside"
on his Army team of the mid-40's. By 1952 Taylor had established herself as a top
star with such films as *Life with Father* (1945) and *A Place in the Sun* (1951).

Kaleidoscope 1945-1952

ACADEMIC AWARDS FOR BEST PICTURE

1945 *The Lost Weekend*
1946 *The Best Years of Our Lives*
1947 *Gentlemen's Agreement*
1948 *Hamlet*
1949 *All the King's Men*
1950 *All About Eve*
1951 *An American in Paris*
1952 *The Greatest Show on Earth*

OTHER POPULAR FILMS

Spellbound (1945)
To Each his Own (1946)
Miracle on 34th Street (1947)
I Remember Mama (1948)
Born Yesterday (1950)
Quo Vadis? (1951)
Showboat (1951)
The Quiet Man (1952)
This Is Cinerama (1952)

Hollywood: Musicals, Brutes & Returning Heroes

The MGM Musical, *An American in Paris*, starring Gene Kelly *(above, left)* and directed by Vincente Minelli, received an Oscar in 1951 for Best Picture and is now considered a classic. Among Kelly's other popular films were *Words and Music* (1948) and *Singing in the Rain* (1952). Burt Lancaster *(above, right)* made his film debut as Swede, a broken-down prizefighter involved with mobsters, in *The Killers* (1946). Also appearing in the screen version of Ernest Hemingway's story were Albert Dekker and Ava Gardner. With Marlon Brando playing Stanley Kowalski, Vivien Leigh won an Oscar for her portrayal of Blanche DuBois *(opposite, top)* in the film version of Tennessee Williams's stage hit, *A Streetcar Named Desire* (1951). Set in the slums of New Orleans, it also starred Kim Hunter. Samuel Goldwyn's *The Best Years of Our Lives* collected nine Academy Awards in 1946, including Best Picture. Directed by William Wyler, the film depicted the return to the same town of three war veterans, a sergeant, an air officer and a sailor. The sergeant, played by Frederic March *(opposite, bottom)*, who won Best Actor, found civilian adjustment easier because of his family, portrayed by Michael Hall and Myrna Loy, with Teresa Wright as the daughter.

Kaleidoscope 1945-1952

POPULAR EARLY TELEVISION SHOWS

Ed Sullivan's *The Toast of the Town*	*I Love Lucy*
The Texaco Star Theatre	*What's My Line?*
The Life of Reilly	*The Lone Ranger*
Your Show of Shows	*See It Now*
The Kraft Television Theatre	*Broadway Open House*
Hopalong Cassidy	*You Bet your Life*
The Firestone Hour	*Playhouse of Stars*
Howdy Doody	*Omnibus*
Kukla, Fran and Ollie	*Your Hit Parade*
Arthur Godfrey's Talent Scouts	*Studio One*

Television began to collect an enthusiastic audience in the late 1940's, and by the early 1950's it was solidly entrenched in American life. Comedy was extremely popular on early television. Milton Berle *(left)*, also called "Mr. Television" and "Uncle Miltie," hosted the first smash television comedy show. His *Texaco Star Theater* began in 1948, and guests on that first show included Pearl Bailey, ventriloquist Señor Wences, and Bill "Mr. Bojangles" Robinson. *Your Show of Shows*, hosted by Sid Caesar, shown here with partner Imogene Coca *(below, left)*, started in 1949 as the *Admiral Broadway Revue*. Produced by Max Liebman, the show made stars out of Caesar, Coca, Carl Reiner, Howard Morris and comedy writer Mel Brooks. Westerns were also popular, including shows by stars Gene Autry, Roy Rogers and Dale Evans, and William Boyd as Hopalong Cassidy *(below, right)*, here shown with a fan in 1950. Not all stars were immediate successes on the new medium, however, especially some who were closely connected with radio. One of these was Ed Wynn, the "Perfect Fool" and the "Fire Chief" *(opposite)*, whose transition to television in 1949, although highly applauded, lasted only two seasons.

22

Kaleidoscope 1945-1952

PULITZER PRIZES FOR FICTION

1945 John Hersey, *A Bell for Adano*
1947 Robert Penn Warren, *All the King's Men*
1948 James A. Michener, *Tales of the South Pacific*
1949 James Gould Cozzens, *Guard of Honor*
1950 A. B. Guthrie, Jr., *The Way West*
1951 Conrad Richter, *The Town*
1952 Herman Wouk, *The Caine Mutiny*

PULITZER PRIZES FOR DRAMA

1945 Mary Chase, *Harvey*
1946 Russel Crouse and Howard Lindsay, *State of the Union*
1948 Tennessee Williams, *A Streetcar Named Desire*
1949 Arthur Miller, *Death of a Salesman*
1950 Richard Rodgers, Oscar Hammerstein II and Joshua Logan, *South Pacific*
1952 Joseph Kramm, *The Shrike*

During World War II, with Paris and its fashions shut off, American women wore spartan styles designed by Americans whose creativity was limited by Government regulations. But after Paris was freed, an unknown French designer named Christian Dior showed a new line of fashionable dresses which, among other things, featured much longer skirts and thinner waistlines. This "New Look" soon swept the United States *(below, left)*. Mississippian William Faulkner *(opposite, top left)* won the 1949 Nobel Prize for literature for such widely acclaimed novels as *Go Down, Moses* (1942) and *Intruder in the Dust* (1948). Dr. Alfred C. Kinsey *(opposite, top right)* interviewed 5,300 American men for his controversial bestseller, *Sexual Behavior in the Human Male* (1948), known popularly as the Kinsey Report. Here, Kinsey interviews a woman for his 1953 book, *Sexual Behavior in the Human Female*. Like Faulkner and the playwrights of the era, Kinsey dealt with sexual relationships not previously discussed openly. The biggest stage success of 1945 was *The Glass Menagerie* by Tennessee Williams *(opposite, bottom)*, here at work on the 1950 film version. Williams's second triumph came in 1947 with *A Streetcar Named Desire*, also a screen hit (see page 21). Another highly successful playwright was Arthur Miller, whose tragic *Death of a Salesman* (1949) *(below, right)* won a Pulitzer Prize.

Kaleidoscope 1945-1952

Gertrude Lawrence,
Mary Martin, Merman & Como

Aside from the few excellent dramatic hits, the most popular stage plays were musicals. Richard Rodgers and Oscar Hammerstein II had first teamed up for an adaptation of an old play called *Green Grow the Lilacs*. Retitled *Oklahoma!*, it became a smash hit (1943). The songs were so enchanting that the original cast recording album (the first ever made of a Broadway show) sold over a million copies. They collaborated successfully again on *Carousel* (1945) and perhaps their finest show, *South Pacific* (1949). Starring Mary Martin as the U.S. Navy nurse, Nellie Forbush *(right)*, and Ezio Pinza as the French planter, Emilie de Becque, the musical was based on James Michener's *Tales of the South Pacific*. Nearly all the songs were popular in their own right, especially "Some Enchanted Evening" and "Bali Ha'i." Two years later the team scored still another hit with *The King and I*, starring Yul Brynner as the King of Siam and Gertrude Lawrence as the English schoolteacher *(below)*. Brynner won a Tony Award for his role in 1952.

In 1946 Irving Berlin had a hit musical in *Annie Get Your Gun*.
Playing sharpshooter Annie Oakley, the brassy-voiced Ethel Merman
(below, left) sang a number of Berlin tunes that became extremely popular,
including "I'm an Indian, Too" and "There's No Business Like Show Business."
Other big musicals included Alan Jay Lerner and Frederick Lowe's story
of a mythical Scottish town, *Brigadoon* (1947), and Cole Porter's *Kiss
Me Kate* (1948). In popular music, the big bands were gradually fading
by the 1950's, and folk music, long popular with many people already,
made an impact on the general music scene. The Weavers *(right)*, a top
folk group, had a big hit in 1951 with "On Top of Old Smoky." Of all
the recording stars in the 1940's and 1950's, Perry Como *(below, right)*,
an ex-barber, was among the most popular. Over 45 of his records made
the hit parade between 1945 and 1952, including "Till the End of Time"
(1945), "Prisoner of Love" (1946), "Because" (1948) and
"Don't Let the Stars Get in Your Eyes" (1952).

Kaleidoscope 1945-1952

Music:
The King & the Duke

TOP SELLING RECORDS

1945 "Till the End of Time" — Perry Como
     "Sentimental Journey" — Les Brown
     "Rum and Coca-Cola" — Andrews Sisters
1946 "The Gypsy" — The Inkspots
     "Rumors Are Flying" — Frankie Carle
     "Oh! What It Seemed to Be" — Frankie Carle
1947 "Near You" — Francis Craig
     "Heartaches" — Ted Weems
     "The Old Lamplighter" — Sammy Kaye
1948 "Buttons and Bows" — Dinah Shore
     "Ballerina" — Vaughn Monroe
     "Mañana" — Peggy Lee
1949 "Riders in the Sky" — Vaughn Monroe
     "That Lucky Old Sun" — Frankie Laine
     "Cruising Down the River" — Russ Morgan
1950 "Goodnight Irene" — Gordon Jenkins and the Weavers
     "The Third Man Theme" — Anton Karas
     "Mona Lisa" — Nat King Cole
1951 "How High the Moon" — Les Paul and Mary Ford
     "The Tennessee Waltz" — Patti Page
     "Because of You" — Tony Bennett
1952 "Cry" — Johnny Ray
     "Wheel of Fortune" — Kay Starr
     "Blue Tango" — Leroy Anderson

Singer Nat "King" Cole (*opposite*) began with a trio but became immensely popular on his own with his romantic, lilting style. Among his top records were "The Christmas Song" (1947), "Nature Boy" (1948), "Mona Lisa" (1950), and "Too Young" (1951). Although the big band sound was beginning to fade, some excellent bands, especially those with a jazz background, continued to have a large following into the 1950's. Among them were the great Duke Ellington (*below*), a composer as well as a performer, and Louis "Satchmo" Armstrong, Benny Goodman, Harry James and Sammy Kaye.

Among the top female vocalists was Dinah Shore *(opposite, top left)* who made the hit parade with "The Gypsy" (1946), "Anniversary Song" (1947), "Buttons and Bows" (1948) and "Sweet Violets" (1951). Tenor Mario Lanza *(opposite, top right)*, here dressed for his starring role in the film *The Great Caruso* (1951), had two of the biggest records of 1951 — "Be my Love" and "The Loveliest Night of the Year." Three enormously successful women were the Andrews Sisters *(opposite, bottom)*, LaVerne,Patty and Maxene, (left to right). They kept the airways and the public dancing before, during and after World War II with, among many other records, "Rum and Coca-Cola" (1945) and "I Can Dream, Can't I" (1949).

In baseball, one of the hottest rivalries was between the New York Yankees and the Brooklyn Dodgers across town. The Dodgers were able to win only one of the seven World Series they played against the Yankees (1955). One of the reasons was the irrepressible Yankee manager Casey Stengel, here discussing pitching with the Duke of Windsor *(right)*. Another baseball hero was Stan "The Man" Musial *(below)*, outfielder for the St. Louis Cardinals. He won the National League's Most Valuable Player award in 1946, was National League batting champion seven times and achieved a lifetime batting average of .331 with 475 home runs. Here, he clouts the 2,000th hit of his career in Philadelphia on September 9, 1952.

WORLD SERIES

(Winners first; number of games last)
(AL - American League; NL - National League)

1945 Detroit Tigers (AL) over Chicago Cubs (NL) (4-3)
1946 St. Louis Cardinals (NL) over Boston Red Sox (AL) (4-3)
1947 New York Yankees (AL) over Brooklyn Dodgers (NL) (4-3)

1948 Cleveland Indians (AL) over Boston Braves (NL) (4-2)
1949 New York Yankees (AL) over Brooklyn Dodgers (NL) (4-1)
1950 New York Yankees (AL) over Philadelphia Athletics (NL) (4-0)
1951 New York Yankees (AL) over New York Giants (NL) (4-2)
1952 New York Yankees (AL) over Brooklyn Dodgers (NL) (4-3)

Major league baseball's color line was broken in 1947 by Jackie Robinson, who was signed by shrewd Dodger general manager Branch Rickey and became Rookie of the Year. The following year at least half a dozen players from the old Negro leagues were signed by the majors, including the great Satchel Paige, who had already played 22 years in the Negro leagues. Here, Robinson slides into second *(top)* with a stolen base in the first game of the 1947 World Series. Professional basketball's first "big man" was George Mikan of the Minneapolis Lakers *(above)*, who won six titles in seven years between 1948 and 1954. College basketball was dominated by the Kentucky Wildcats and coach Adolph Rupp *(right)*, who led his teams to four N.C.A.A. championships.

Courage and determination marked two of the greatest golfers of the 1940's and 1950's. Ben Hogan *(below, left)* was winner of many tournaments in the late 1940's, including the U.S. Open and the P.G.A. twice. Then a tragic auto accident in 1949 suddenly seemed to end his golfing career. But the Texan overcame his pain and came back in 1950 to win the U.S. Open a second time. Hogan was visibly limping with pain during the 1952 and 1953 tournaments, yet he won the Masters, the U.S. Open and the British Open all in 1953. His skill and determination won him nine major career victories, six of them after his near-fatal accident. Mildred "Babe" Didrikson Zaharias *(below, right)* has won more titles in more sports than any other athlete, including males. The Associated Press voted her the Woman Athlete of the Half Century in 1950 for her Olympic gold medals, world records in track and field, and other honors in softball and basketball. But golf was her favorite sport, and in 1947 she was the first American to win the British Women's Amateur championship, following that with sixteen consecutive tournament victories in the U.S. Then in 1953 she had a cancer operation and was told she would never be able to compete again. But she won seven more tournaments before her death in 1956.

Kaleidoscope 1945-1952

One of the greatest of all Olympic athletes, Bob Mathias was only a California high schooler of 17 when he competed in the Olympic Games in London in 1948. In spite of age, inexperience and wet weather, he won the tough decathlon far in front of the nearest competitor. In the 1952 games in Helsinki, Mathias *(top left)*, here completing the 1,500-meter race, won the decathlon an unprecedented second time with an even greater number of points than in 1948. Tennis greats Ted Schroeder *(in foreground, top right)* and defending champion Pancho Gonzales met for the 1949 U.S. Men's Singles championship at Forest Hills, New York. Gonzales overcame early losses and retained his title by beating Schroeder in the last three of the five sets. In boxing *(opposite)*, Joe Louis (on right) retained his heavyweight championship against challenger Billy Conn at New York's Yankee Stadium in June 1946; a record $100 was charged for each ringside seat. Louis was impressive throughout the fight and finally KO'd Conn in the eighth round. The first thoroughbred to earn over a million dollars, Citation *(above)*, here winning the 1948 Kentucky Derby, could win on any track and easily captured the 1948 Triple Crown with jockey Eddie Arcaro.

The top college football teams in the country in the late 1940's were undisputedly Army, Notre Dame and Michigan. The Army team, led by Heisman Trophy winners Felix "Doc" Blanchard and Glenn Davis (see page 18), "Mr. Inside" and "Mr. Outside" of football, went unbeaten for 28 games in the years 1944-1946. Taking a cue from the Black Knights, Notre Dame, coached by Frank Leahy, went unbeaten for 39 games from 1946 to 1950. Irish quarterback Johnny Lujack *(left)* was an All-American in 1946 and 1947. The Michigan Wolverines under coach H.O. "Fritz" Crisler *(below, left)* went 25 games without a loss in the years 1946-1949. But talent was not limited to the stadiums. Bess Myerson *(below)* was crowned Miss America in Atlantic City, New Jersey, in September 1945. Unlike many other winners of this title who faded from public view, Myerson became a well-known television personality, consumer advocate, journalist, educator and volunteer administrator.

HEISMAN TROPHY WINNERS

1945 Felix Blanchard, Army, fullback
1946 Glenn Davis, Army, halfback
1947 John Lujack, Notre Dame, quarterback
1948 Doak Walker, Southern Methodist, halfback
1949 Leon Hart, Notre Dame, end
1950 Vic Janowicz, Ohio State, halfback
1951 Richard Kazmaier, Princeton, halfback
1952 Billy Vessels, Oklahoma, halfback

Professional football, too, had many great teams and players. One of the greatest was the Philadelphia Eagles' powerful running back Steve Van Buren *(above, left)*. As the National Football League's top rusher four times in the late 1940's, Van Buren led the Eagles to the N.F.L. championship twice. "Slingin" Sammy Baugh *(above, right)* of the Washington Redskins was the league's leading passer four times in the late 1940's. He was so confident of his passing accuracy that he sparked the Redskins to an N.F.L. championship his first year as a pro (1937). Other football greats were Sid Luckman, quarterback for the powerhouse Chicago Bears; quarterback Otto Graham of the Cleveland Browns, which won six consecutive conference championships in the early 1950's; and receiver Elroy "Crazy Legs" Hirsch of the Los Angeles Rams, who popularized the "bomb" (long scoring pass) and who, with teammate Tom Fears, was half of the best receiving team in pro football history.

NATIONAL FOOTBALL LEAGUE CHAMPIONS

(Winners first; scores last)
(EC - Eastern Conference;   WC - Western Conference)

1945 Cleveland Rams (WC) over
          Washington Redskins (EC) (15-14)
1946 Chicago Bears (WC) over
          New York Giants (EC) (24-14)
1947 Chicago Cardinals (WC) over
          Philadelphia Eagles (EC) (28-21)
1948 Philadelphia Eagles (EC) over
          Chicago Cardinals (WC) (7-0)
1949 Philadelphia Eagles (EC) over
          Los Angeles Rams (WC) (14-0)
1950 Cleveland Browns (EC) over
          Los Angeles Rams (WC) (30-28)
1951 Los Angeles Rams (WC) over
          Cleveland Browns (EC) 24-17
1952 Detroit Lions (WC) over
          Cleveland Browns (EC) (17-7)

Some of the period's biggest news
stories were reported by CBS newsman
Edward R. Murrow *(opposite)*, who, along with
Walter Winchell, had one of the most recogni-
zable news voices on the air. Murrow's dramatic
broadcasts from bombed London during World War II
(always commencing "This is London....") gave him
an international reputation, and in 1951 he
began his *See It Now* television program, following
it two years later with *Person to Person*. In
the 1950's he gained fame and admiration as
an undaunted opponent of Senator Joseph McCarthy.
Schoolchildren and New Yorkers *(right and
below)* could not wait for official confirmation
of the end of war in Europe and joyously
celebrated victory on May 7, 1945.

Kaleidoscope 1945-1952   *Crime & Independence*

Nazi leaders from the broken Third Reich were
tried for war crimes by an international tribunal in
1945 and 1946 in Nuremburg, Germany, the greatest
war trial in history. Sentencing was stern: Ten of
the Nazis were hanged and twelve were imprisoned.
Among other Nazis seated at the final session in January 1946 *(opposite, top)* were, front row, left to
right, Field Marshal Hermann Göring, Rudolf Hess,
Foreign Minister Joachim von Ribbentrop and Field
Marshal Wilhelm Keitel. In September 1948, Germans
in Berlin watched as a U.S. supply plane landed at
Templehof Airport to help the beleaguered city *(above)*
in the third month of the Berlin airlift. The Soviet
military government in occupied Germany had begun
a land blockade of Berlin's Allied sectors on June 24.
In ceremonies in New Delhi on August 19, 1947 *(right,
center)*, Viscount Mountbattan, the last Governor-
General of India, administered the oath of office
to Jawaharlal Nehru as the first premier of free
India. But there were many bitter feelings between
the Muslims and the Hindus that often led to violence.
The most shocking single act of violence was the
assassination on January 20, 1948, of the "father
of India," Mahatma Gandhi, by an extremist Hindu.
Three days later *(right, bottom)*, Gandhi lay in
state in New Delhi. In New York in March 1951,
(opposite, bottom), the Senate Crime Committee, with
Senator Estes Kefauver (third from left) as chairman,
began its televised hearings on organized crime.
Underworld figure Frank Costello (second from right)
faced intensive questioning from the committee.

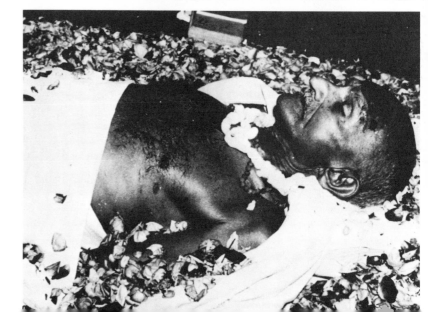

David Ben-Gurion proclaimed the
establishment of the new state of Israel
(left) in ceremonies in Tel Aviv on May 14,
1948. The historic building is now a museum.
National Chinese troops left Shanghai in 1949
(below, left), retreating from advancing Communist Chinese armies. Before the year was out,
Chiang Kai-shek had moved the Nationalist
government to Taiwan (Formosa), leaving the
mainland to Mao Tse-tung's Communists.
Senator Joseph McCarthy *(below, right)*, gained
a huge following beginning in 1950 for his
mostly unfounded accusations of Communists
in Government. McCarthy's star began to fade
in 1954 at the Army-McCarthy hearings, but
accusations of infiltrating Communists continued until the late 1950's. British royalty
(opposite) as well as the world mourned the
death of King George VI on February 6, 1952.
Queen Mary *(center)* stood with the Queen
Mother Elizabeth and the new Queen Elizabeth
II, awaiting the beginning of lying-in-state
ceremonies in Westminster Hall, London.

1945
The Decision

The Big Three — Winston Churchill, President Truman and Joseph Stalin — met at Potsdam, Germany, in July to discuss the postwar world. It was the first time Truman and Stalin met face-to-face and Truman saw for himself an Iron Curtain in the making.

The year 1945 was probably the most momentous one in the history of the United States since the nation's birth, and it certainly was a turning point in world history. It was Harry S. Truman, who became President in April, who led the American people — and to a considerable extent, the entire free world — through it. Roosevelt had told him nothing about the prosecution of the war. He had never been in the White House War Room. He hadn't heard about the atomic bomb, while Joseph Stalin, Soviet dictator, knew almost everything about it.

So the new President started from scratch. On April 25, almost two weeks after he was sworn in, Truman finally received a briefing on the development of a nuclear weapon, the same day as the San Francisco Conference establishing the United Nations opened. On May 1, Adolph Hitler's death was announced. Seven days later, on the President's sixty-first birthday, he proclaimed V-E Day, the end of war

in Europe, to the nation. On July 15, the President arrived in Europe for the Potsdam Conference between the Big Three powers to discuss the shape of the postwar world. The following day he was informed that an atomic device had been exploded successfully in the desert about fifty miles from Alamogordo, New Mexico.

The President had been giving careful thought to the question of using the bomb against the Japanese and he consulted a wide range of eminent advisors, political, scientific and military. He made the final decision to go ahead and use the bomb while still in Potsdam. His decision was based on the calculation that, in the long run, using it would save lives, Japanese as well as American. General George C. Marshall had estimated that if we had to invade the Japanese homeland, a half-million American lives would be lost. The Japanese, in their fanatic defense of their sacred home soil, would lose even more, perhaps many millions. A fire raid on Tokyo by American bombers using conventional weapons caused the deaths of 78,650 Japanese — more than either atomic bomb killed; and undoubtedly many more raids of this kind would have to be undertaken if the atomic bomb was not used.

Thus individual bombs were dropped on Hiroshima (August 6) where 60,175 were killed and on Nagasaki three days later, destroying another 35,000 people. But then the killing was over. Japan surrendered on August 14.

Assuming Role as President

. . . The reason for this invitation is the fact that in 1945 I was presiding over the Senate of the United States as Vice President. The Senate adjourned at 5:00. I had an engagement to see the Speaker on a matter that was pending in both houses in which the administration was interested. When I got to the Speaker's office I didn't have a chance to talk to him but was instructed to return a call from the White House, which I did. I was informed by Mr. Steve Early, who was at that time the President's secretary, that he would like to see me at the White House at the main entrance as soon as I could get there. I had not much of an idea of what I would be faced with when I arrived. I was informed by Mrs. Roosevelt that the President had passed away, and I immediately asked her if there was anything I could do for the family. And she very kindly and courteously told me that there was nothing at that time, that it was not herself and her family that needed help but it was the former Vice President that needed help.

The chief justice was summoned and eight and a half to nine minutes after seven o'clock on the [evening] of April 12, I was sworn in as President of the United States.

I want it very clearly understood that on my part there is no celebration on this day. It is a day of sadness for me because we lost on this day four years ago Franklin D. Roosevelt, I think one of the greatest Presidents this country has ever had.

Impromptu Speech to Senate
(April 12, 1949)

. . . It would have been very foolish not to realize that President Roosevelt was a very sick man. It became perfectly obvious to me that due to [his] health I would eventually inherit the Presidency. I had seen him just thirteen days

before. His eyes were sunken, his magnificent smile was missing from his careworn face. He seemed a spent man.

I realized that I would probably have to take over an impossible job, and I had a strange feeling that Mr. Roosevelt knew.

Television Interview
(December 15, 1964)

Our departed leader never look backward. He looked forward and moved forward. That is what he would want us to do. That is what America will do. . . .

I humbly pray Almighty God, in the words of King Solomon, "Give therefore thy servant an understanding heart to judge thy people, that I may discern between good and bad: for who is able to judge this thy so great a people?" I ask only to be a good and faithful servant of my Lord and my people.

First Speech to Congress
April 16

Ending the War

The world may be sure that we will prosecute the war on both fronts, East and West, with all the vigor we possess, to a successful conclusion.

First Official Pronouncement
April 12

This is not the hour for final victory in Europe, but the hour draws near. . . . The last faint, desperate hope of Hitler and his gangster government has been extinguished. . . . The junction of our forces at this moment signalizes to ourselves and to the world that the collaboration of our nations in the cause of peace and freedom is an effective collaboration which . . . will succeed.

On Meeting of U.S. and U.S.S.R. Armies in Germany
April 27

United, the peace-loving nations have demonstrated in the West that their arms are stronger by far than the might of dictators or the tyranny of military cliques that once called us soft and weak. . . . For the triumph of spirit and of arms which we have won, and for its promise of peoples everywhere who join us in the love of freedom, it is fitting that we as a nation give thanks to Almighty God, who has strengthened us and gives us the victory.

V-E Day Proclamation
May 8

1945

President Roosevelt and Vice President Truman lunched together *(opposite)* in early 1945. Truman believed that F.D.R. was one of the best presidents America ever had. After F.D.R.'s death, Truman was sworn in as President *(above)* on April 12 in the White House, while his wife and daughter looked on.

47

I am getting ready to see Stalin and Churchill and it is a chore. I have to take my tuxedo, tails, preacher coat, high hat, low hat and hard hat.

Letter to his Mother (Before leaving for Potsdam Conference)
July

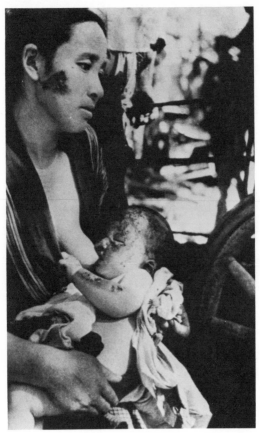

We have just dropped a bomb on Japan which has more power than 20,000 tons of TNT. It was an overwhelming success.

. . . What has been done is the greatest achievement of organized science in history. . . . The fact that we can release atomic energy ushers in a new era in man's understanding of nature's forces.

Announcement of First Use of Atomic Bomb
August 6

We have used it [atomic bomb] in order to shorten the agony of war, in order to save the lives of thousands and thousands of young Americans. . . .

Radio Speech on War Developments (Berlin Conference)
August 9

As President of the United States, I had the fateful responsibility of deciding whether or not to use the atom bomb for the first time. It was the hardest decision I ever had to make. But the President cannot duck hard problems — he cannot

1945

Truman called his decision to use the
atomic bomb on Japan one of the hardest he
ever had to make. For a single piece of equipment,
the new weapon was tremendously powerful — first
an enormous fireball *(opposite, top)*, then a
slowly forming cloud of radioactive material
(right). Hiroshima was in ruins after the first
blast *(below)*, and Japanese civilians struggled
for survival *(opposite, bottom)*. Three days
later, a second bomb destroyed Nagasaki, but
neither blasts were as destructive as the
incendiary raids on Tokyo months earlier.

Although Truman had seen Churchill before becoming President, the meeting at Potsdam *(right)* was the first time they had conferred. Both men liked each other immediately. Later, in Berlin, Truman joined General Dwight Eisenhower *(below)* for a ceremonial raising of the flag that had flown over the U.S. Capitol on December 7, 1941.

pass the buck. I made the decision after discussions with the ablest men in our Government, and after long and prayerful consideration. I decided that the bomb should be used in order to end the war quickly and save countless lives — Japanese as well as American. But I resolved then and there to do everything I could to see that this awesome discovery was turned into a force for peace and the advancement of mankind. Since then, it has been my constant aim to prevent its use for war and to hasten its use for peace.

(October 14, 1948)

. . . It is our responsibility — ours the living — to see to it that this victory shall be a monument worthy of the dead who died to win it. . . . This is a victory of liberty over tyranny. . . .

We now know that the spirit of liberty, the freedom of the individual and the personal dignity of man are the strongest and toughest and most enduring force in all the world. . . .

V-J Day Proclamation
September 2

. . . I recommend that Congress adopt legislation combining the War and Navy Departments into one single department of national defense. . . . It is now time . . . to provide for the future the soundest, the most effective and the most economical kind of structure for our armed forces. . . .

Speech to Congress Asking Unification of Armed Services
December 19

The United Nations

The world has experienced a revival of an old faith in the everlasting moral force of justice. . . . I earnestly appeal to each and every one of you to rise above personal interests and adhere to those lofty principles that benefit all mankind. . . . We must work and live to guarantee justice — for all. . . .

You members of this conference are to be the architects of the better world. . . . We still have a choice between the alternatives: the continuation of international chaos — or the establishment of a world organization for the enforcement of peace. . . .

We were not isolated during the wars, we dare not become isolated in peace. . . . In order to have good neighbors we must be good neighbors. . . . All progress begins with dif-

ferences of opinion and moves onward as the differences are adjusted through reason and mutual understanding. . . . If we do not want to die together in war, we must live together in peace. . . . We must build a new world—a far better world — one in which the eternal dignity of man is respected.

Address to Opening of U.N. Conference in San Francisco
April 25

. . . The charter of the United Nations which you are now signing is a solid structure upon which we can build for a better world. . . . It [charter] was proof that nations, like men, can state their differences, can face them, and then can find common ground on which to stand. That is the essence of democracy. . . . The world has learned again that nations, like individuals, must know the truth if they would be free — must read and hear the truth, learn and teach the truth. . . . Upon all of us, in all of us, in all our countries, is now laid the duty of transforming into action these words which you have written.

Address to Final Session, U.N. Conference
July 26

A Free Press

. . . The American free press, through the stress of the most horrible of all wars, withstood subservience and open attack and operated under a voluntary code of censorship. . . . Ours, then, is the plain duty . . . to make a free press the true torch of world peace.

Message for National Newspaper Week
September 27

. . . Our resources have barely been touched. Some of our natural resources, lumber, for instance, have been exhausted by senseless deforestation. . . . We created the greatest production machine in the history of the world. . . . We must keep that machine operating. . . .

Dedication of Kentucky Dam
October 10

. . . Artistic talent is not the exclusive property of any one race or group. One of the marks of democracy is its willingness to respect and reward talent without regard to race or origin.

Letter to D.A.R. Condemning Prejudice in Refusing Use
of their Hall to Negro Pianist
October 12

When I hear Republicans say I'm doing all right, I know damned well I'm wrong.

Speech at Kansas City

. . . We should resolve now that the health of the nation is a national concern; that financial barriers in the way of attaining health should be removed; that the health of all its citizens deserves the help of all the nation.

Speech to Congress on National Health Program
November 1⁰

1946
A Nation Divided

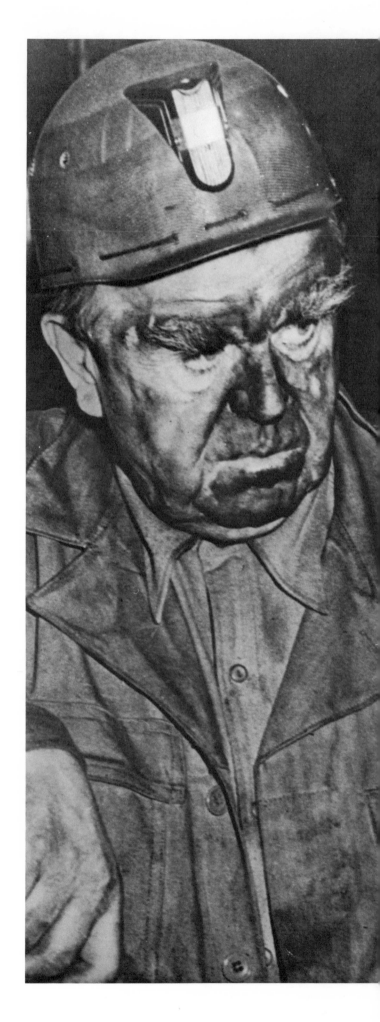

The year after the war ended brought an end to the spirit of cooperation that, during the war, had been maintained between labor and management, liberals and conservatives, Democrats and Republicans. President Truman was in the middle of these conflicts as the nation attempted to determine the shape of the postwar world.

The President wanted to lift wartime controls gradually. Republicans, however, supported by most of the nation's businessmen, wanted to get rid of price controls immediately and return to unbridled free enterprise and they were successful. Controls were lifted and prices soared. The labor unions were also spoiling for fights as the War Labor Act expired and labor once again had the right to strike. During the first full year after the war five million men went on strike. Truman was equally opposed to the turmoil and disruption, as well as inflation, this caused.

In May, as a railway strike was threatened, the President signed an executive order whereby the Federal Government seized the railroads. A few days later, while the President was addressing Congress, asking for a law allowing him to draft into the army all railroad workers who went on strike, the unions agreed to a settlement. A note telling of this was handed to the President as he delivered his address to Congress. He stopped in mid-sentence to announce: "Gentlemen, the strike has been settled."

His showdown with John L. Lewis, boss of the United Mine Workers, began in May, when the President seized the coal mines and gave the U.M.W. most of what they wanted, thus ending a forty-day work stoppage. But Lewis was eager to challenge the President again, and on a minor pretext, he called his men out again in November. The crucial day came on December 4 when a Federal judge fined Lewis $10,000 and the union $3,510,000, the heaviest fine in labor history. The union immediately said that they would appeal to the Supreme Court. But after the President announced that he would broadcast an appeal to the miners over their leader's head, asking them to go back to work (and only hours before the broadcast was scheduled), Lewis capitulated and he had the miners return. The President's victory was complete.

That victory, however, came too late to prevent the defeat at the polls for the Democrats in early November. The American people, angered and frustrated by soaring inflation, shortages, strikes and slowdowns chose the President as a scapegoat. The Republicans — using the slogan, "Had enough?" — took control of Congress for the first time in sixteen years. Unknown to the President or anyone, this Congress was to give him his best issue and winning slogan in the 1948 Presidential campaign.

President Truman's showdown with United Mine Workers head, John L. Lewis *(opposite)*, reached a climax in December when Lewis's union was given the heaviest fine in labor history — $3,510,000. In New York on October 23, Truman met with Soviet Foreign Minister Molotov *(below)* at a reception for United Nations delegates convening in the U.S. for the first time. General Harry Vaughn, the President's military aide, looked on.

Economic and Labor Turmoil

I wish I could say to you that everything is in perfect order — that we are on the way to eternal prosperity. I cannot. . . . In order to give a fact-finding board a reasonable chance to function before a strike is actually called, I suggested that there be a thirty-day "cooling off period." . . . Production is the greatest weapon against inflation. . . .

Of the three major components which make up our standard of living — food, clothing and housing — housing presents our most difficult problem. . . . We urgently need about five million additional homes — now. . . .

The problems of our economy will not be solved by timid men, mistrustful of each other. . . . When we turn to our domestic problems we do not find a similar record of achievement [as in foreign affairs] and progress in Congress.

Broadcast to American People
January 3

. . . Unless the Price Control Act is renewed there will be no limit to which our price levels would soar. Our country would face a national disaster. . . . There is no question in my mind that the government, acting on behalf of all the people, must assume the ultimate responsibility for the economic health of the nation. There is no other agency that can. . . . During this trial war the voices of disunity were silent or were subdued. . . . Those voices are beginning to cry aloud again. We must learn constantly to turn deaf ears to them.

State of Union and Budget Message
January 21

My fellow countrymen — I come before the American people tonight at a time of great crisis [threatened railroad strike].

The crisis of Pearl Harbor was the result of action by a foreign enemy. The crisis tonight is caused by a group of men within our own country who place their private interests above the welfare of the nation. . . .

I assume that these two men [union leaders Johnston and Whitney] know the havoc which their decision has caused, and the even more extreme suffering which will result in

the future. . . . This is no contest between labor and management. This is a contest between a small group of men and their Government. . . .

If sufficient workers to operate the trains have not returned by 4 p.m. tomorrow, as head of your Government I have no alternative but to operate the trains by using every means within my power. . . .

This emergency is so acute and the issue is so vital that I have requested the Congress to be in session tomorrow at 4 p.m. and I shall appear before a joint session of the Congress to deliver a message on this subject [requesting power to draft railroad workers into the army].

Radio Address
May 24

. . . Unless the railroads are manned by returning strikers, I shall immediately undertake to run them by the Army of the United States. . . . This is no longer a dispute between labor and management. It has now become a strike against the Government of the United States itself. . . . I request temporary legislation to take care of this immediate crisis. I request permanent legislation leading to the formulation of a long-range labor policy designed to prevent the recurrence of such crises and generally to reduce the stoppages of work in all industries for the future. . . . Strikes against the Government must stop. . . . As a part of this temporary emergency

President Truman conferred with his aides. Photographs of the Truman family can be seen on the desk at right, and a lithograph of the U.S.S. Frigate *Missouri* on the wall (see page 8).

1946

legislation I request the Congress immediately to authorize the President to draft into the armed forces of the United States all workers who are on strike against their Government.

Plea to Congress for Railroad Strike Action
May 25

Reporter: Mr. President, do you have any plans to seize the Pittsburgh ball club?
Truman: The Pittsburgh ball club goes on strike?
Reporter: They are going to go out tomorrow night.
Truman: Well, I want to say to you that if those ball fellows go on strike, and I have to take them over, I'll have two damn good teams in St. Louis.

June 6

Well, I had to fire Henry today and, of course, I hated to do it. If Henry had stayed as Secretary of Agriculture in 1940 as he should have, there'd never have been all the controversy and I would not be here and wouldn't that be nice? Charley Ross said I'd rather be right than President and I told him I'd rather be anything than President.

Well, now he's out, and the crackpots are having conniption fits. I'm glad they are. It convinces me I'm right.

Letter to his Mother (After Firing Henry Wallace
as Secretary of Commerce)
September

Keeping the Peace

. . . The country was brought through four years of peril by an effort that was truly national in character. . . . To achieve success will require both boldness in setting our sights and caution in steering our way on an uncharted course. . . . The spectacular progress of science . . . has speeded internal development and changed world relationships so fast that we must realize the fact of a new era. . . . We face a great peacetime venture; the challenging venture of a free enterprise economy making full and effective use of the rich resources and technical advances. . . .

We will not measure up to those responsibilities by the simple return to "normalcy" that was tried after the last war. . . . Industrial peace between management and labor will have to be achieved. . . . It is the government's responsibility to see that our economic system remains competitive, that new businesses have adequate opportunities and that our national resources are restored and improved.

. . . Our most immediate task . . . is to deprive our enemies completely and forever of their power to start another war. Of even greater importance to the preservation of international peace is the need to preserve the wartime agreement of the United Nations and to direct it into the ways of peace.

. . . It is the hope of all Americans that in time future historians will speak not of World War I and World War II, but of the first and last world wars.

State of Union and Budget Message
January 21

. . . We must remain strong because only so long as we remain strong can we ensure peace in the world. Peace has to be built on power for good. . . . From the military point of view, how can we best maintain this strength and leadership? . . . First, unification of all our armed services in a single department; second, temporary extension of the Selective Service Act; and third, universal training.

. . . The same unswerving determination and effort which produced the release of atomic energy can and will enable mankind to live without terror and to reap untold benefits from this new product of man's genius.

Army Day Address
April 6

. . . If there is no understanding, there can be no peace; and if there is no education, there can be no peace. . . . There are two things in the world I want above everything else — peace in the world and unity at home. . . . You can make that contribution on a world basis. I want you to do it.

Greeting Delegates of National Commission on
Educational, Scientific and Cultural Cooperation
September 25

Religion in America

. . . Here, as perhaps nowhere else in the world, the fundamental unity of Christianity and freedom has been demonstrated. . . . Religion in America is a supreme demonstration of unity in diversity. . . . The atomic bomb . . . ended one age and began another: the new and unpredictable age of the soul.

Message to General Assembly of Presbyterian Church
May 18

"ONE LITTLE THING — BEFORE HE THROWS OUT THE FIRST BALL, THE PRESIDENT WONDERS IF YOU WOULD BE KIND ENOUGH TO POINT OUT A REPUBLICAN . . ."

A *Chicago Sun-Times* cartoon *(left)* emphasized Truman's ebullience. The President walked with Eleanor Roosevelt *(above)* during a visit to the Roosevelt home at Hyde Park, New York. Truman held the former First Lady in the highest esteem for her selfless social work and her interest in government.

1946

. . . International dealings are no different from those carried on among individuals. . . . There isn't any more reason why we can't understand each other as nations than why we can't understand each other as individuals.

Now it is your duty, as the educators of the country, to get the rising generation to believe that; and if you can overcome those prejudices which cause wars — religious prejudices, economic prejudices, misunderstandings between roles and people of different languages — we can accomplish this. . . . Unless we have a code of morals which respects the other fellow's interests and in which we believe that we should act as we would be acted by, you can never maintain peace. . . . When a man wants an education badly enough, he usually manages to get it; but it has been our system to make it easy for him to get that education, and we want that to continue. . . .

Address to American Council on Education
July 11

. . . We have found that it is easier for men to die together on the field of battle than it is for them to live together at home in peace. . . . We have our unique national heritage because of a common aspiration to be free and because of our purpose to achieve for ourselves and our children the good things of life which the Christ declared he came to give to all mankind.

Christmas Address
December 24

The ballot is both a right and a privilege. The right to use it must be protected and its use by everyone must be encouraged. Lastly, every veteran and every citizen, whatever his religion or his national origin, must be protected from all forms of organized terrorism.

Wire to N.A.A.C.P.
June 26

. . . Those who truly desire to see the fullest expression of our democracy can never rest until the opportunity for an education, at all levels, has been given to all qualified Americans, regardless of race, creed, color, national origin, sex or economic status. . . . Yet in this country today there exists disturbing evidence of intolerance and prejudice similar in kind, though perhaps not in degree, to that against which we fought the war. Discrimination, like a disease, must be attacked wherever it appears.

Letter to Chairman of American Veterans Committee
September 4

In a ceremony at the White House, President Truman signed one of the many bills Congress presented him during his years in office. But because of labor troubles, the Republicans won control of Congress in the November elections, for the first time in eleven years.

1947
The Cold War

Early 1947 marked the point at which the United States assumed active leadership of the anti-Communist forces of the Cold War. The Greek monarchy was engaged in a severe struggle with Communist guerrilla forces who were being supplied by Communist neighbors. Soon after Turkey's non-aggression pact with the Soviet Union expired in 1945, the Russians began pressuring that nation to yield bases in and near the strategically crucial Bosporus and Dardanelles, entrances to the Black Sea.

On February 24, President Truman received a note from the British ambassador that Britain would withdraw all support of Greece by March 30. The President had to decide within days whether or not to allow Greece and Turkey to fall to Soviet imperialism and to have the Communists perhaps control much of the eastern Mediterranean. He knew that if he decided to help these countries he would have to struggle with the Republican-controlled Eightieth Congress which still contained many isolationists, but he soon concluded that the United States should give Greece and Turkey whatever they needed, for, as he stated in his *Memoirs*, "the alternative would be disastrous to our security and to the security of free nations everywhere." The plan that became known as the Truman Doctrine was announced to Congress on March 12.

The Cold War

. . . This is an age when unforeseen attack could come with unprecedented speed. We must be strong enough to defeat, and thus to forestall, any such attack. . . . We have made it clear to all nations that the United States will not consent to [peace] settlements at the expense of principles we regard as vital to a just and enduring peace. We have made it equally clear that we will not retreat to isolationism. . . . The spirit of the American people can set the course of world history. . . . But there are ways of disagreeing; men who differ can still work together sincerely for the common good. We shall be risking the nation's safety and destroying our opportunities for progress if we do not settle any disagreements in this spirit, without thought of partisan advantage.

State of the Union Address
January 6

The very existence of the Greek state is today threatened by the terrorist activities of several thousand armed men, led by Communists, who defy the government's authority at a number of points, particularly along the northern boundaries. A commission appointed by the United Nations Security Council is at present investigating disturbed conditions in northern Greece on the one hand and Albania, Bulgaria and Yugoslavia on the other.

Meanwhile, the Greek government is unable to cope with the situation. The Greek army is small and poorly equipped. It needs supplies and equipment if it is to restore the authority of the government throughout Greek territory.

Greece must have assistance if it is to become a self-supporting and self-respecting democracy. The United States must supply this assistance. . . .

There is no other country to which democratic Greece can turn.

. . . The United Nations and its related organizations are not in a position to extend help of the kind that is required.

. . . The government of Greece is not perfect. Nevertheless, it represents 85 percent of the members of the Greek parliament who were chosen in an election last year. Foreign ob-

Truman believed in freedom of the press and accommodated reporters and photographers, although frequently they received some of his well-aimed barbs. Once when a reporter asked him if he had seen any flying saucers, Truman replied, "Only in the newspapers."

servers, including 692 Americans, considered this election to be a fair expression of the views of the Greek people.

As in the case of Greece, if Turkey is to have the assistance it needs, the United States must supply it. . . .

I believe that it must be the policy of the United States to support free peoples who are resisting attempted subjugation by armed minorities or by outside pressures. I believe that we must assist free peoples to work out their own destinies in their own way. I believe that our help should be primarily through economic and financial aid which is essential to economic stability and orderly political processes. . . .

If we falter in our leadership, we may endanger the peace of the world — and we shall surely endanger the welfare of this nation.

Speech to Congress on New Foreign Policy
(Truman Doctrine)
March 12

The Western Hemisphere cannot alone assure world peace, but without the Western Hemisphere no peace is possible. . . . It is for us, the young and the strong, to erect the bulwarks which will protect mankind from the horrors of war forever.

Address at Close of Rio Conference
September 2

1947

Winston Churchill visited Truman *(above)* at his home in Independence. In a speech at Fulton, Missouri, Churchill first used the term "Iron Curtain." President Truman awarded a service medal to retiring General George C. Marshall *(opposite)* in late 1945. Marshall then became Truman's Secretary of State and later Secretary of Defense. Truman believed that Marshall was one of the greatest Americans of the twentieth century.

. . . We must decide whether or not we will complete the job of helping the free nations of Europe to recover from the devastation of the war. . . . If Europe fails to recover, the peoples of these countries might be driven to despair — the philosophy which contends that their basic wants can be met only by the surrender of their basic rights to totalitarian control. Such a turn of events would constitute a shattering blow to peace and stability in the world. . . .

Message to Congress Asking $17 Million for Marshall Plan
December 19

Inflation and Prosperity

. . . The job at hand today is to see to it that America is not ravaged by recurring depressions and long periods of unemployment, but that instead we build an economy so fruitful, so dynamic, so progressive that each citizen can count upon opportunity and security for himself and his family.
. . . The long-range agricultural policy of the Government should be aimed at preserving the family-sized farm and preventing another agricultural depression. . . .

Economic Report to Congress
January 8

. . . We are viewing a panorama of prosperity — such prosperity as no generation of Americans before us ever experienced. . . . If we abandon our work of reclamation, of soil conservation, of preserving our forests, of developing our water resources, we are wasting money, not saving it. If we cease our vigilance along the borders of our country and at our ports of entry, we are wasting money, not saving it. If we falsely economize by reducing the staff of men and women who audit tax returns, or who increase the country's productivity by settling labor disputes, we are wasting money, not saving it. If we cut down the effectivness of our armed forces, we run the risk of wasting both money and lives.

Jefferson Day Dinner Address
April 5

. . . I know the worries of a breadwinner whose earnings cannot keep up with the high cost of living . . . I know how hard it is to skimp and save, and do without. . . . We could wait until depression caught up with us, until our living standards sank, and our people tramped the streets looking for jobs. . . . That would be the course of defeatism and cowardice. Our other course is to take timely and forthright action. If we do this we can hold the spiral of inflation at home, relieve hunger and cold abroad, and help our friendly neighbors become self-governing once again.

Radio Address on Special Congressional Session
October 24

Conservation

. . . Without regard for sectional rivalries or for party politics, the nation has advanced constantly in the last seventy-five years in the protection of its natural beauties and wonders. . . . Each national park possesses qualities distinctive enough to make its preservation a matter of concern to the whole nation. . . .

We cannot afford to conserve in a haphazard or a piece-meal manner. . . . If we waste our minerals by careless mining and processing, we shall not be able to build the machinery to till the land. If we waste the forests by careless lumbering, we shall lack housing and contruction materials for factory, farm and mine. If we waste the water through failure to build hydroelectric plants, we shall burn our reserves of coal and oil needlessly. If we waste our soil through erosion and failure to replenish our fields, we shall destroy the sources of our people's food.

. . . The battle for conservation cannot be limited to the winning of new conquests. . . . There are always plenty of hogs who are trying to get our natural resources for their own personal benefit. . . . For conservation of the human spirit, we need places . . . where we may be more keenly aware of our Creator's infinitely varied, infinitely beautiful, and infinitely bountiful handiwork.

Address at Dedication of Everglades National Park
December 6

. . . In time of peace as in time of war, our ultimate strength stems from the vigor of our people. . . . At no time can we afford to lose the productive energies and capacities of millions of our citizens. Nor can we permit our children to grow up without a fair chance of survival and a fair chance for a healthy life. . . . We must not reserve a chance of good health for the well-to-do alone. . . .

National health insurance is the most effective single way to meet the nation's health needs. . . . Until it is a part of our national fabric we shall be wasting our most precious national resource and shall be perpetuating unnecessary misery and human suffering.

Message to Congress on Federal Health Program
May 19

. . . And our schools have made much progress in supplying the constant stream of thoughtful, educated men for public service called for by President Cleveland half a century ago. . . . In the present critical stage of world history, we need, more than ever before, to enlist all our native integrity and industry in the conduct of our common affairs. . . . Our schools must train future leaders in all fields to understand and concern themselves with the expanded role of government, and — equally important — to see the need for effective administration of the Government's business in the public interest. . . . They [universities] should develop in their students the capacity for seeing and meeting social problems as a whole and for relating special knowledge to broad issues.

Address at Princeton University's Bicentennial
June 17

I have just made some additions to my Kitchen Cabinet, which I will pass on to my successor in case the cow should fall down when she goes over the moon.

I appointed a Secretary for Inflation. I have given him the worry of convincing the people that no matter how high the

prices go, nor how low wages become, there just is not any danger to things temporal or eternal. I am of the opinion that he will take a real load off my mind — if Congress does not.

Then I have appointed a Secretary of Reaction. I want him to abolish flying machines and tell me how to restore oxcarts, oar boats and sailing ships. What a load he can take off my mind if he will put the atom back together so it cannot be broken up. . . .

I have appointed a Secretary for Columnists. His duties are to listen to all radio commentators, read all columnists in the newspapers from ivory tower to lowest gossip, coordinate them and give me the result so I can run the United States and world as it should be. . . .

I have appointed a Secretary of Semantics — a most important post. He is to furnish me with 40 to 50 dollar words. Tell me how to say yes and no in the same sentence without a contradiction. He is to tell me the combination of words that will put me against inflation in San Francisco and for it in New York. He is to show me how to keep silent — and say everything. You can very well see how he can save me an immense amount of worry.

Memorandum

1947

President Truman reviewed photographs *(opposite)* of an important conference. Truman looked forward to his visits home, away from the formality of the White House. Such visits always included seeing neighbors and friends, whether on the streets or at the Jackson County Fair *(above)*.

1948
Giving 'Em Hell

As the 1948 Democratic National Convention approached in July, the situation couldn't have seemed worse for the party and for Harry Truman. One commentator said his influence was weaker at the time than that of any other modern President. The Republicans had just nominated an experienced campaigner, Governor Thomas E. Dewey of New York, with an efficient, well-financed organization behind him. The President was opposed by the nation's press and his own party was split between the Progressives on the left, led by Henry A. Wallace, whom Truman had fired as Secretary of Commerce in 1946, and the States' Rights "Dixiecrats" on the right, led by J. Strom Thurmond, Governor of South Carolina. Even some of those who stayed within the main stream of the party wanted Truman to bow out so that General Dwight Eisenhower, war leader and now President of Columbia University, could

have the nomination. Shortly before the convention, however, Eisenhower unequivocally said he would reject the nomination if offered. Many other faithful Democrats who liked Truman thought he had no chance to win the election. On top of everything else, the party had no money.

But Truman won the nomination, rather easily as it turned out, and he gave a rousing acceptance speech that set the tone for the campaign. As he told his running mate, Senator Alben Barkley, "I'm going to fight hard, I'm going to give them hell." And he did.

A memo from Truman's political strategy board summed up the uphill campaign facing him: "This election can be won only by bold and daring steps calculated to reverse the powerful trend now running against us." In his acceptance speech the President announced he would call a special session of Congress to enact legislation he considered to be needed des-

Just elected for his first full term as President in what was called the upset of the century, Truman held up an erroneous newspaper headline *(opposite)* on the back of his campaign train — possibly the most famous Truman photo. Earlier, during the height of the campaign, a Herblock cartoon in the *Washington Post (below)* assailed the Republicans.

perately by the country, dealing with issues such as inflation controls, public housing and civil rights. Many of the things he asked for were supported by the Republican platform. When the Republicans failed to pass anything of substance in the twelve-day session, Truman achieved his real purpose in calling the session: He pointed out the hypocrisy of the Republican platform and he focused attention on the "Do-Nothing" Eightieth Congress, which became his best campaign issue.

This was followed up, beginning in September, with a series of extensive whistle-stop tours of the nation aboard the "Truman Special." Since the President's delivery from prepared texts was frequently stiff and unpersuasive, on these tours he ad-libbed all but a few major addresses. He was also provided with "tour books" which contained some basic information about each stop, however brief, so that Truman could say something appropriate and complimentary about the local area. He combined these elements with a slashing attack on the Republicans, calling them "the Wall Street reactionaries," "gluttons of privilege," and telling the farmers in Iowa that the Republican Congress had "stuck a pitchfork" in their backs. But it is essential to note that Truman never did this in a vicious way. His style was to say these things in a somewhat jocular, only half-serious manner, much as someone might talk to a friend informally.

The crowds that came out to hear the President were large and generally enthusiastic, and consistently exceeded in size those of Governor Dewey who chose to ignore the issues Truman raised. Instead, Dewey spoke philosophically and sedately in unctuous tones about entering, "on January 20," (inauguration day) "upon a new era." Acting as if he had already been elected, Dewey stressed unity and limited himself to generalities. Truman, emanating the image of the game underdog, called these speeches "mealy-mouthed." Traveling 22,000 miles and making 270 speeches, the President's energy never flagged, although everyone else on his campaign train was frequently exhausted.

The newspaper columnists and editorial writers believed that a Dewey victory was a foregone conclusion. On the day before the election, the Gallup Poll gave Dewey 49.5 percent of the vote, Truman 44.5; Elmo Roper gave Dewey 52.2 percent, Truman 37.1. But when the votes were counted a few hours later, the President had won reelection. Forever afterward, underdog Presidential candidates would remind the voters of the year Harry Truman pulled the biggest upset of all time.

The Presidential Campaign

. . . I'm exceedingly anxious to see the Republican platform for 1948. You know they've been in the habit since 1936 of taking a few planks out of the old Democratic platforms and building a platform and then saying "Me, too."

. . . I want to say to you that for the next four years there will be a Democrat in the White House and you're looking at him. . . .

I've often wondered what a so-called liberal Republican thinks. . . . I wish I could explain to you how they [Republicans] have bungled the budget in every particular. . . . I wish I could explain to you how they've hampered the enforcement of the law, how they made a phony cut in the Treasury Department. . . . Oh, I wish we had an Isaiah or a Martin Luther to lead us out of this moral despond into which we have fallen.

Address to Young Democrats
May 14

The President is virtually in jail. He goes from his study to his office and from his office to his study, and he has to have guards there all the time. And they do a good job, too — I am not criticizing the guards — but when you get out and see people and find out what people are thinking about, you can do a better job as President of the United States.

June 4

. . . There is the big white jail.

Comment on Passing by the White House
(April 13, 1958)

Senator Barkley and I will win this election, and make these Republicans like it, don't you forget that. We'll do that because they're wrong and we're right. . . .

[The Democratic Party has] been elected four times in succession and I'm convinced it will be elected a fifth time next November. The reason is that the people know the Democratic Party is the people's party, and the Republican Party is the party of special interests and it always has been and always will be. . . .

The Republican Party favors the privileged few and not the common, everyday man. Ever since its inception, that party has been under the control of special privilege, and they concretely proved it in the Eightieth Congress. . . . They proved it by the things they failed to do. [Two of the greatest failures of the Republican Congress were] of major concern to every American family: the failure to do anything about high prices, and the failure to do anything about housing.

[While the Republican platform asked for the extension and increase of Social Security benefits, when the Republicans actually had the power] they took 750,000 people off our Social Security rolls. I wonder if they think they can fool the people with such poppycock as that. . . .

My duty as President requires that I use every means within my power to get the laws the people need on matters

1948

A Truman supporter (*above*) dressed up for the Democratic Convention in Philadelphia during the summer. Although television was still new, Truman used the medium to advantage during his campaign (*opposite*).

of such importance and urgency. . . . On the twenty-sixth day of July, which out in Missouri they call Turnip Day, I'm going to call the Congress back and I'm going to ask them to pass laws halting rising prices and to meet the housing crisis which they say they're for in their platform. At the same time I shall ask them to act on other vitally needed measures such as aid to education, which they say they're for; a national health program, civil rights legislation, which they say they're for; an increase in the minimum wage, which I doubt very much they're for; funds for projects needed in our program to provide public power and cheap electricity, . . . an adequate and decent law for displaced persons in place of the anti-Semitic, anti-Catholic law which this Eightieth Congress passed. . . .

If there is any reality behind that Republican platform, we ought to get some action out of the short session of the Eightieth Congress. They could do this job in fifteen days if they wanted to do it. . . . What that worst Eightieth Congress does in its special session will be the test. The American people will decide on the record.

Acceptance Speech,
Democratic National Convention, Philadelphia
July 15

. . . In this critical [world] situation, my motto has been: Keep your temper and stand firm. . . . His [the farmer's] great danger is that he may be voted out of a fair deal and into a Republican deal. . . . The Republican strategy is to divide the farmer and the industrial worker and business and get them to squabbling with each other so they can grasp the balance of power and take the country over, lock, stock and barrel. . . . The Republican gluttons of privilege are cold men.

Address at Dexter, Iowa
September 18

. . . Republicans in Washington have a habit of becoming curiously deaf to the voice of the people. . . . But they have no trouble at all hearing what Wall Street is saying.

Speech at Denver
September 20

A woman called to Truman while he was campaigning, "President Truman, you sound as if you had a cold."

He replied, "That's because I ride around in the wind with my mouth open."

The Republican leadership wouldn't give the American people the kind of housing they need because the rich real estate lobby opposed it. The Hoover slogan, if you remember, back in 1929 and 1930 was, "Two cars in every garage." The Republican slogan today is, "Two families in every garage."

October 7

. . . The Republicans have the propaganda and the money, but we have the people, and the people have the votes.

Speech at Akron, Ohio
October 10

They [Republicans] favor the minimum wage — the smaller the minimum the better. . . . They think the American standard of living is a fine thing — as long as it doesn't spread to all the people. . . . They admire the Government of the United States so much that they would like to buy it.

Speech at St. Paul, Minnesota
October 13

. . . I'm a home-grown American farm product. And I'm proud of the breed I represent — the completely unterrified form of American democracy. . . . I don't think you have to be hit on the head twice to know who hit you the first time.

Speech at North Carolina State Fair
October 19

I never give them hell. I just tell the truth and they think it is hell.

Explaining his "Give 'em Hell" Speeches

Polls are like sleeping pills designed to lull the voters into sleeping on Election Day. You might call them "sleeping polls."

October 26

. . . We have two great goals — one to build a secure life for ourselves here at home and the other to build a lasting peace for the world. . . . And now, my fellow citizens, the future welfare of our country is in your hands.

Final Radio Address to Voters
November 1

. . . The victory was not my victory but a victory of the Democratic Party for the people.

November 3

1948

During the campaign, local politicians and townspeople turned out wherever the "Truman Special" stopped *(above)*. Cartoonist Le Baron Coskley of the *National CIO News* chided fellow journalists and the "political experts" *(opposite)* on their prediction of Truman's political demise.

International Crises

. . . We have never shut the door against any country. We are willing to talk peace and international intercourse with any country in the world, but we will not stand idly by and see the liberties of the world debauched.

Criticizing U.S.S.R. at American Hellenic Educational and
Progressive Association Banquet
March 29

Reporter: Mr. President, did Dr. Weizmann suggest a loan to Israel?
Truman: He did not suggest a loan. He said he would like to have a loan, just like every other country. If you know of any countries that wouldn't like to have a loan, I wish you would name them.

May 27

. . . Anyone can talk of peace. But only the work that is done for peace really counts. . . . We fought through World War II with only one purpose: to destroy the tyrants who tried to impose their rule on the world and enslave its peoples. We sought no territories; we asked for only token reparations. At the end of the war we quickly dismantled the greatest military machine ever built by any nation. . . .

Why, then, after such great exertions and huge expenditures, do we live today in a twilight period — between a war so dearly won and a peace that still eludes our grasp? The answer is not hard to find. It lies largely in the attitude of one nation — the Soviet Union. . . . It has intervened in the internal affairs of many other countries by means of Communist parties directed from Moscow. . . . The refusal of the Soviet Union to work with its wartime allies for world recovery and world peace is the most bitter disappointment of our time. . . . We have no hostile or aggressive design against the Soviet Union or any other country. We are not waging a "cold war." . . .

The cleavage that exists is not between the Soviet Union and the United States. It is between the Soviet Union and the rest of the world. . . . No nation has the right to exact a price for good behavior. . . . We refuse to play fast and loose with man's hope for peace. . . . The only prize we covet is the respect and goodwill of our fellow members of the family of nations.

Address at University of California
June 12

[President Truman once told V. M. Molotov, the Soviet Union's Foreign Minister, that honoring the agreements made between the allied nations at Yalta was not a one-way street. He pointed out that the U.S. and the United Kingdom respected every Yalta covenant, but that the Soviets had not done so, using Poland as an example.]
Molotov: I have never been talked to in my life like this.
Truman: Carry out your agreements and you won't get talked to like this.

WS OF HIS DEATH GREATLY EXAGGERATED!

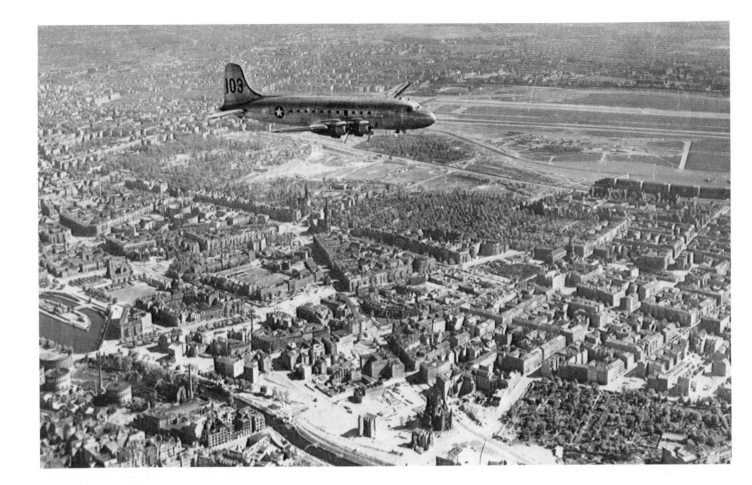

. . . The first and most important feature of our foreign policy is to strengthen the United Nations. . . . Our guiding principle is international cooperation. . . . In my search for peace I do not care what epithets may be hurled at me by those who think that we must hurry on to inevitable catastrophe.

Speech at Brooklyn
October 29

Civil Rights

. . . We believe that all men should have a voice in their government and that government should protect, not usurp, the rights of the people. . . . There is a serious gap between our ideals and some of our practices. This gap must be closed. . . . The protection of civil rights begins with the mutual respect for the rights of others which all of us should practice in our daily lives. . . . The protection of civil rights is the duty of every government which derives its power from the consent of the people. . . .

I recommend, therefore, that the Congress enact legislation . . . establishing a permanent Commission on Civil Rights, a Joint Congressional Committee on Civil Rights and a Civil Rights Division in the Department of Justice. . . .

We know that our democracy is not perfect. But we do know that it offers a fuller, freer, happier life to our people than any totalitarian nation has ever offered.

Message to Congress on Civil Rights
February 2

1948

The blockade of Berlin by the Russians began on June 19, and the Berlin airlift *(above)* began soon after. Much of Berlin was still in ruins, including the famous Kaiser Wilhelm Church (in foreground), now standing as a memorial. Soviet-controlled German police carefully checked each vehicle entering or leaving the Russian sector of Berlin, especially at the primary checkpoint at Brandenburg Gate *(opposite)*.

. . . We are interested in the security and welfare of the family, because that is the fundamental unity on which all governments are formed. . . . Children and dogs are as necessary to the welfare of this country as is Wall Street and the railroads, or any one of them. . . .

The President may have a great many powers given to him in the Constitution and may have powers under certain laws which are given to him by the Congress of the United States; but the principal power that the President has is to bring them in and try to persuade them to do what they ought to do without persuasion. . . . The President can't solve problems by himself. The Congress can't solve problems, but the President and the Congress and the country can solve any problem that comes before us.

Speech to National Conference on Family Life
May 6

. . . The Communists, both here and abroad, are counting on our present prosperity turning into a depression. They do not believe that we can — or will — put the brake on high prices. They are counting on economic collapse in this country. . . . The vigor of our democracy is judged by its ability to take decisive actions. . . .

Address to Extra Session of Congress
July 27

1949 A Pact to Prevent War

Over a year of extensive Presidential effort was required to make the North Atlantic Treaty Organization a reality. For Truman it was the next logical step, a monumentally crucial one, beyond the Marshall Plan. Once Western Europe had recovered economically, with America's help, from World War II, it was necessary for the same nations to form a strong military alliance, again with America as the bulwark, for mutual protection.

But until 1949, the United States had never had a peacetime military alliance. The President spent many long hours in the spring of 1948 working with Undersecretary of State Robert M. Lovett and Senator Arthur Vandenberg, a Republican from Michigan, to change the minds of several recalcitrant men in Congress who saw no need to depart from the path set by George Washington in his famous Farewell Address when he urged the United States to avoid "entangling alliances." To President Truman and others with foresight that viewpoint no longer made sense in a world that had become small through the development of jet-powered aircraft, long-range rockets and instant worldwide communications, and infinitely more dangerous because of the atomic bomb. No nation, not even the United States, could remain isolated.

When the Republican Senate passed the Vandenberg Resolution in June of 1948, Senator Vandenberg correctly described its acceptance as "the most important step in American foreign policy since the promulgation of the Monroe Doctrine." When the final treaty was signed on April 4, 1949, the President, in a typical gesture of humility, insisted that it should be signed for the United States by the man who had done the most work toward its acceptance — Secretary of State Dean Acheson — while the President and Vice President stood at his side.

Thus we made known to the Soviet bloc that America and its allies were determined to defend Western Europe against aggression such as that which devoured the Republic of Czechoslovakia in February of 1948 when the Communists staged a successful coup d'etat. The President recognized from experience that the Russians respected only force, and now the free nations of N.A.T.O. had the economic and military strength and unity to negotiate with the Communists as equals.

Within two and a half months of the signing of the N.A.T.O. treaty, the President presented still another imaginative proposal to help contain Communism on a worldwide front — the Point-Four programs to bring American technical skill, rather than its money, to the aid of the underdeveloped nations, so that they could join the twentieth century and avoid the tentacles of Soviet imperialism. The takeover of mainland China by Mao Tse-tung's Communist forces at the end of 1949 reinforced the President's determination.

One of Truman's most monumental tasks
was completed on April 4 in the State
Department auditorium in Washington —
the signing of the North Atlantic Treaty.
Over a year of Presidential work had gone
into N.A.T.O.'s foundation and Truman believed
it was among his best accomplishments.
Truman spoke to the various foreign ministers
and ambassadors before the signing,
which was done for the U.S. by Dean Acheson,
seen here immediately right of center.

Defense Against Communism

. . . I accept with humility the honor which the American people have conferred upon me. . . . The United States and other like-minded nations find themselves directly opposed by a regime with contrary aims and a totally different concept of life. That regime adheres to a false philosophy which purports to offer freedom, security and greater opportunity to mankind. . . . That false philosophy is Communism. . . . Communism is based on the belief that man is so weak that he is unable to govern himself, and therefore requires the rule of strong masters. Democracy is based on the conviction that man has the moral and intellectual capacity, as well as the inalienable right, to govern himself with reason and justice.

. . . In the coming years our program for peace and freedom will emphasize four major courses of action. First, we will continue to give unfaltering support to the United Nations. . . . Second, we will continue our programs for world economic recovery. . . . Third, we will strengthen freedom-loving nations against the dangers of aggression. . . . Fourth, we must embark on a bold new program for making the benefits of our scientific advances and industrial progress available for the improvement and growth of underdeveloped areas. . . . The old imperialism — exploitation for foreign profit — has no place in our plans.

. . . Slowly but surely we are weaving a world fabric of international security and growing prosperity. . . . Our allies are the millions who hunger and thirst after righteousness. . . . In due time . . . I believe that those countries which now oppose us will abandon their delusions and join with the free nations of the world in a just settlement of international differences. . . . But I say to all men, what we have achieved in liberty, we will surpass in greater liberty.

Inaugural Address
January 20

. . . It is altogether appropriate that nations so deeply conscious of their common interests should join in expressing their determination to preserve their present peaceful situation and to protect it in the future. . . . We are like a group of householders living in the same locality, who decide to express their community of interests by entering into a formal association for their mutual self-protection. . . .

There are those who claim that this treaty is an aggressive act on the part of the nations which ring the North Atlantic. That is absolutely untrue. The pact will be a positive, not a negative, influence for peace. . . . For us, war is not inevitable. We do not believe that there are blind tides of history which sweep men one way or another.

Signing of the North Atlantic Treaty
April 4

The grinding poverty and the lack of economic opportunity for many millions of people in the economically underdeveloped parts of Africa, the Near and Far East, and certain regions of Central and South America, constitute one of the greatest challenges of the world today. In spite of their age-old economic and social handicaps, the peoples in these areas have, in recent decades, been stirred and awakened. The spread of industrial civilization, the growing understanding of modern concepts of government, and the impact of two world wars have changed their lives and their outlook. They are eager to play a greater part in the community of nations.

All of these areas have a common problem. They must create a firm economic base for the democratic aspirations of their citizens. Without such an economic base, they will be unable to meet the expectations which the modern world has aroused in their peoples. If they are frustrated and disappointed, they may turn to false doctrines which hold that the way of progress lies through tyranny. . . .

For these various reasons, assistance in the development of the economically underdeveloped areas has become one of the major elements of our foreign policy. In my inaugural address, I outlined a program to help the peoples of these areas to attain greater production as a way to prosperity and peace.

The major effort in such a program must be local in character; it must be made by the people of the underdeveloped areas themselves. It is essential, however, to the success of their effort that there be help from abroad. . . .

The aid that is needed falls roughly into two categories. The first is the technical, scientific, and managerial knowledge necessary to economic development. . . .

The second category is production goods — machinery and equipment — and financial assistance in the creation of productive enterprises. . . .

It has already been shown that experts in these fields can bring about tremendous improvements. For example, the health of the people of many foreign communities has been greatly improved by the work of United States sanitary engineers in setting up modern water supply systems. The food supply of many areas has been increased as the result of the

1949

Bess Truman *(opposite)* was an admirable
First Lady who disliked publicity because she
didn't like people to "make a fuss" over her.
Vice President Alben Barkley often conferred
with Truman *(above)* on foreign affairs, going
overseas to gather firsthand information.

advice of United States agricultural experts in the control
of animal diseases and the improvement of crops. These
are only examples of the wide range of benefits resulting
from the careful application of modern techniques to
local problems. . . .

Point-Four Program Message to Congress
June 24

Planning the Economy

The reactionaries hold that government policies should be
designed for the special benefit of small groups of people who
occupy positions of wealth and influence. Their theory seems
to be that if these groups are prosperous, they will pass along
some of their prosperity to the rest of us. This can be
described as the "trickle-down theory."

November 3

We have abandoned the "trickle-down" concept of national
prosperity. . . . The American people have decided that
poverty is just as wasteful and just as unnecessary as pre-
ventable disease. . . .

As we look around the country many of our shortcomings stand out in bold relief. . . . Each of these shortcomings is also an opportunity.

. . . Our first great opportunity is to protect our economy against the evils of "boom and bust." . . . We cannot afford to float ceaselessly on a postwar boom until it busts. . . . Minimum wage fixed by law should be raised to at least 75 cents an hour. . . . We must assure small business the freedom and opportunity to grow and prosper. . . .

Standard of living on the farm should be just as good as anywhere else. Farm price supports are an essential part of our program to achieve these ends. . . .

Here we are now with a new start. All I want to do is carry out the will of the people of the United States. . . . I want a fair deal for every part of the population of this great nation. . . .

State of the Union Address
January 5

. . . When we talk about planning the things we want to do economically we are charged with being Communists and fellow-travelers. . . . The people who find fault with us . . . are thinking about controlled economy, not planned economy. . . . And I imagine that unless the people are fully informed as to what the efforts are, we ought to put forth for that sort of planning. We will have the usual result of nothing accomplished. . . .

Speech to National Planning Association
February 1

... Farmers and industrial workers — agriculture and industry — ought to show their products together. . . . No program for prosperity in the country can ignore the interests of either group. . . . The special interests always fail to see that the way of progress, the way of greater prosperity for themselves, as well as others, lies in the direction of a fuller and happier life for all.

Labor Day Address, Pittsburgh
September 5

The Job of the Presidency

. . . I have always been an optimist. I have always believed that right will prevail. I have labored under the idea that if the people of the country understand clearly what the issues were in the campaign, they would only vote one way. . . .

I have always said that I am sure there are a million men in the United States, no doubt, who could do the job much better than I can or could do it. But I have the job, and I have to do it, and the rest of you have got to help me.

Speech to Democratic National Finance Committee
January 19

The President spends most of his time kissing people on the cheek in order to get them to do what they ought to do without getting kissed. . . . I work only eighteen hours a day now. Maybe I can put in twenty now. . . . I wish I could stay longer but I have to go back and put in four more hours to make up my eighteen hours.

Speech to National Planning Association
February 1

Once upon a time, there were a number of citizens who thought that Andrew Jackson ought to have a suitable coffin. At great expense, they went to Syria and purchased a marble sarcophagus. A sarcophagus, as you know, is a tomb — a big marble coffin with a marble lid. These citizens then shipped this box to Washington, which was quite a job, as it weighed four or five tons.

At last, they thought, a suitable resting place had been provided for Andrew Jackson.

Well, the only trouble with the project was that Andrew Jackson wasn't dead. Moreover, he wasn't ready to die. And he did not intend to be hurried to his grave.

Courteously but firmly, he wrote to these well-meaning citizens and said, "I must decline the intended honor."

And they never did get Old Hickory into that thing. . . . Andy wouldn't even be buried in it.

I think that this little story has a moral in it. It is this: Before you offer to bury a good Democrat, you'd better be sure he is dead.

Speech at Jefferson-Jackson Day Dinner, Washington
February 24

Reporter: Mr. President, the first thing Jefferson did [regarding the alien and sedition laws] was to release eleven newspaper publishers from prison.

Truman: Yes, I think he made a mistake on that.

June 16

1949

In June Truman joined fellow members of his old 35th Division in a reunion parade in Little Rock, Arkansas *(opposite)*. Cartoonist Dorman H. Smith portrayed *(below)* the Republicans shut out of the White House for the seventeenth year.

1950
Land War in Asia

The Truman policy of containing Communism received its severest test in 1950. The Communists in Asia made their aggressive move only six months after pushing Chiang Kai-shek's army out of mainland China. On June 25, 1950, the army of Communist North Korea struck across the border at the thirty-eighth parallel to invade the Republic of South Korea. Surprised, outnumbered and inadequately equipped, the South Koreans were able to offer little effective resistance.

Two days later the U.N. Security Council adopted a United States' resolution urging member states to furnish the assistance necessary to enable South Korea to repel the armed attack. That same day President Truman authorized the use of American air and naval forces to support the South Koreans, describing this as a "police action" rather than as an act of war which Congress would have to approve, although it eventually did so anyway. President Truman later called his decision to enter the Korean conflict a most difficult one. In his *Memoirs* he tells of his thoughts soon after learning of the invasion. He remembered how, in the 1930's, the lack of forceful response from the democracies to aggression against Manchuria, Austria and Ethiopia encouraged the Axis Powers to start World War II.

On July 8, General Douglas MacArthur was named U.N. Commander in Korea, but by August 5, American ground forces had been driven into a small perimeter around the port of Pusan on the southeast coast. In mid-September the Americans staged a brilliant amphibious operation at Inchon, catching the North Koreans by surprise. At the same time, the American Eighth Army launched an offensive from

Pusan, and the North Korean Army began to disintegrate. By October 26 the U.N. troops had swept northward through North Korea to the Yalu River, which marks part of the border between China and North Korea.

At about the same time advance U.N. units came into contact with the first Communist Chinese troops, and a month later, 300,000 Chinese "volunteers" attacked. The Eighth Army was forced to withdraw and, by December 15, they occupied a position generally along the thirty-eighth parallel. The next day President Truman declared a national state of emergency.

As the end of the year approached, the President jotted down his ominous thoughts at random: "I have worked for peace for five years and six months and it looks like World War III is near." Within hours of the arrival of the new year of 1951 in the United States the Chinese Communists sent 500,000 men against the U.N. lines.

Korea

. . . I have ordered the United States air and sea forces to give the Korean government troops cover and support. The attack upon Korea makes it plain beyond all doubt that Communism has passed beyond the use of subversion to conquer independent nations and will now use armed invasion and war. It has defied the orders of the Security Council of the United Nations issued to preserve international peace and security. . . .

Statement on Korea
June 27

. . . At 4:00 o'clock in the morning, Sunday, June 25, Korean time, armed forces from north of the thirty-eighth parallel invaded the Republic of Korea. . . . The reports from the [U.N.] Commission [on Korea] make it unmistakably clear that the attack was naked, deliberate, unprovoked aggression, without a shadow of justification. . . . The attack on the Republic of Korea, therefore, was a clear challenge to the basic principles of the United Nations charter and to the specific actions taken by the United Nations in Korea. If this challenge had not been met squarely, the effectiveness of the United Nations would have been all but ended, and the hope of mankind that the United Nations would develop into an institution of world order would have been shattered.

The vigorous and unhesitating action of the United Nations and the United States in the face of this aggression met with an immediate and overwhelming response throughout the free world. The first blow of aggression had brought dismay and anxiety to the hearts of men the world over. . . . This united and resolute action to put down lawless aggression is a milestone toward the establishment of a rule of law among nations.

. . . The attitude of the Soviet government toward the aggression against the Republic of Korea is in direct contradiction to its often-expressed intention to work with other nations to achieve peace in the world. . . . It should be made perfectly clear that the action was undertaken as a matter of basic moral principle. . . . Our assistance to the Republic of Korea has prevented the invaders from crushing the nation in a few days as they had evidently expected to do. . . . With peace re-established, even the most complex political questions are susceptible of solution.

On October 15, President Truman met with his Far East commander, General Douglas MacArthur (opposite), on Wake Island in the Pacific to discuss MacArthur's public disagreement with Truman's foreign policy. At the end of the year, the conflict in Korea intensified (below) with the addition of Red Chinese troops against the U.N. forces.

. . . I shall not attempt to predict the course of events. But I am sure that those who have it in their power to unleash or withhold acts of armed aggression must realize that new recourse to aggression in the world today might well strain to the breaking point the fabric of world peace. . . . We are concerned with advancing our prosperity and our well-being as a nation, but we know that our future is inseparably joined with the future of other free peoples.

Message to Congress on Korea
July 19

. . . Korea is a small country, thousands of miles away, but what is happening there is important to every American. . . . The free nations have learned the fateful lesson of the 1930's. That lesson is that aggression must be met firmly. Appeasement leads only to further aggression and ultimate war. . . .

. . . There are three things we need to do. First, we need to send more men, equipment and supplies to General MacArthur. Second, in view of the world situation, we need to build up our own army, navy, and air force over and above what is needed in Korea. Third, we need to speed up our working with other countries in strengthening our common defenses.

. . . We know that the cost of freedom is high. But we are determined to preserve our freedom — no matter what the cost. . . .

Television Statement on Korea
July 19

I pinned a medal on General MacArthur the other day, and told him I wished I had a medal like that, and he said that it was my duty to give medals, not to receive them. That is always the way. About all I receive are the bricks. It's a good thing I have got a pretty hard head, or it would have been broken a long time ago.

October 21

Point-Four Program

Propaganda is one of the most powerful weapons the Communists have in this struggle. . . . This propaganda can be overcome by truth — plain, simple, unvarnished truth. . . . If they are given the true facts these falsehoods become laughable instead of dangerous.

. . . Everywhere that the propaganda of Communist totalitarianism is spread, we must meet it and overcome it with honest information about freedom and democracy. . . . At the same time, we must overcome the constant stream of slander and vilification that the Communists pour out in an effort to discredit the United States and other free nations. . . . We must strive constantly to break down or leap over barriers to free communication wherever they exist. . . . We have tremendous advantages in the struggle for men's minds. We have truth and freedom on our side.

Address to American Society of Newspaper Editors
April 20

1950

Nationalist Chinese President Chiang Kai-shek and his wife greeted fellow countrymen *(opposite)* in Taipei, Taiwan (Formosa), shortly after the Communists had driven his forces from mainland China. A U.S. soldier in Korea grimaced *(below)* as he fired a 75mm recoilless rifle.

. . . It took two world wars to bring home to us the fact that world distances have disappeared. We are next-door neighbors now to people in other countries who once were scarcely more than names to us. We have become citizens of a larger community — the whole world.

. . . It is the great problem — and the great challenge of our age — that strangers have become fellow-citizens at a time when the world is so deeply divided. . . . We have become neighbors of a new and terrible tyranny.

. . . How do we meet this overriding problem — the most important one of our time? . . . First, we cannot compromise our own moral and ethical beliefs. . . . Second, we cannot isolate ourselves. . . . We can do this: We can, together with other nations of the free world, clearly demonstrate the superiority of the ideals of freedom over the iron hand of tyranny. . . . Point Four provides an example of broad-scale collective action on the part of many countries to bring the benefits of better living conditions to individuals now suffering from ill health, illiteracy and poverty. The Point-Four program is one of the greatest contributions we can make to the course of freedom.

Address at Laramie, Wyoming
May 9

. . . I had a card from Los Angeles this morning, in which the writer suggested to me in all seriousness that the proper thing to do was to surrender to Russia. He said we may lose

our freedom but it is better to lose our freedom than to lose our lives. Now, what do you think of that? That is Patrick Henry in reverse if I know anything.

Address to Conference on Citizenship, Washington, D.C.
May 23

If you tell Congress everything about the world situation, they get hysterical. If you tell them nothing, they go fishing.

July 17

Internal Security

. . . Justice is the foundation of true democracy. Our system of justice preserves the freedom and dignity of the individual, and his right to think and speak as he feels and to worship as he pleases. . . .

Against this tyrannical force, which we know as Communism, the United States stands as a great champion of freedom. . . . The real danger is that Communism might overrun other free nations and thus strengthen itself for an ultimate attack upon us. . . . This administration has fought Communism with action and not just words. . . . There is no area of American life in which the Communist party is making headway, except maybe in the deluded minds of some people.

. . . I set up the employee loyalty program three years ago with two objectives in mind. I was determined . . . to see that no disloyal person should be employed by our Government. . . . I was equally determined that loyal Government employees should be protected against accusations which were false. . . . The preservation of the strictest confidence with respect to loyalty files is the single most important element in operating a loyalty program. . . . Disclosure of the files would result in serious injustice to the reputation of many innocent persons.

. . . Our attack on Communism is embodied in a positive threefold program: One, we are strengthening our own defenses and aiding free nations in other parts of the world so that they can effectively resist Communist aggression. Two, we are working to improve our democracy so as to give further proof, both to our own citizens and to people in other parts of the world, that democracy is the best system of government that men have yet devised. Three, we are working quietly but effectively, without headlines of hysteria, against Communist subversion in this country, wherever it appears, and we are doing this within the framework of the democratic liberties we cherish.

. . . We are not going to transfer our fine F.B.I. into a gestapo secret police. . . . We are not going to try to control what our people read and think. We are not going to turn the United States into a Right-Wing totalitarian country to deal with a Left-Wing totalitarian threat.

Address to Federal Bar Association
April 24

1950

On November 1, two Puerto Rican nationalists tried to shoot their way into the Blair House in Washington, D.C., to assassinate President Truman. Security guards returned the fire, killing one of the nationalists and wounding the other *(opposite)*. One guard was also killed. The First Family was staying in the Blair House while the White House was being renovated. Like any President, Truman had enemies, but he was well-known for his jovial and ready smile *(above)*.

In brief, when all the provisions of H. R. 9490 are considered together, it is evident that the great bulk of them are not directed toward the real and present dangers that exist from Communism. Instead of striking blows at Communism, they would strike blows at our own liberties and at our position in the forefront of those working for freedom in the world. At a time when our young men are fighting for freedom in Korea, it would be tragic to advance the objectives of Communism in this country, as this bill would do. . . .

Insofar as the bill would require registration by the Communist party itself, it does not endanger our traditional liberties. However, the application of the registration requirements to so-called Communist-front organizations can be the greatest danger to freedom of speech, press and assembly, since the alien and sedition laws of 1798. This danger arises out of the criteria or standards to be applied in determining whether an organization is a Communist-front organization.

There would be no serious problem if the bill required proof that an organization was controlled and financed by the Communist party before it could be classified as a Communist-front organization. However, recognizing the difficulty of proving those matters, the bill would permit such a determination to be based solely upon "the extent to which the positions taken or advanced by it from time to time on matters of policy do not deviate from those" of the Communist movement.

. . . Our position in the vanguard of freedom rests largely on our demonstration that the free expression of opinion, coupled with government by popular consent, leads to national strength and human advancement. Let us not, in cowering and foolish fear, throw away the ideals which are the fundamental basis of our free society.

Veto of McCarran Internal Security Act in Message to Congress
September 22

Law Enforcement

. . . We must use our courts, and our law enforcement agencies and the moral forces of our people to put down organized crime wherever it appears. At the same time, we must aid and encourage gentler forces to do their work of prevention and cure.

. . . The most important business in this nation — or in any other nation for that matter — is raising and training children. . . . I don't think we put enough stress on the necessity of implanting in the child's mind the moral code under which we live. . . . Above all, we must recognize that human misery breeds most of our crime. . . . We must teach that we should do right because it is right, and not in the hope of any material reward.

I believe that as President it is necessary for me to be more careful in obeying the laws than for any other person to be careful. I never infringe a traffic rule. I never exercise the perogatives I sometimes have of going through red lights.

Address to Meeting of Law Enforcement Officers
February 15

. . . The nation's welfare requires that soft coal production be resumed at once, in order to prevent human suffering and disastrous economic disallocation. . . . Therefore, I recommend that the Congress enact legislation authorizing the Government to take over the coal mines and operate them temporarily as a public service.

Statement on Seizure of the Striking Coal Mines
March 3

About the meanest thing you can say about a man is that he means well.

May 10

[Referring to a bill be vetoed on the last possible day, although he had intended all along to veto it, President Truman said he felt like the blacksmith on the jury in Missouri who, when the judge asked him if he felt any prejudice against the defendent, replied:] "Oh, no, Judge, I think we should give him a fair trial, then I think we ought to take the s.o.b. out and string him up."

June 26

. . . It is essential to the national defense and the security of the nation, to the public health, and to the public welfare generally that every possible step be taken by the Government to assure to the fullest possible extent continuous and uninterrupted transportation service. Accordingly, I intend to take all steps necessary to assure the continual operation of the railroads.

Statement on Seizure of the Striking Railroads
August 25

1950

Truman stopped in Honolulu *(below)* in October while on his way to Wake Island to meet MacArthur. He later conferred *(opposite)* with British Prime Minister Clement Attlee at the White House, along with Secretary of State Dean Acheson and Secretary of Defense George Marshall. Attlee succeeded Churchill as Prime Minister during the Potsdam Conference in 1945 when his Labour Party won elections.

. . . Both Hawaii and Alaska are vital to the defense of the United States in the Pacific. They are also the proving ground of our democratic institutions in the Pacific area, with tremendous psychological influence on the hearts and minds of the people of Asia and the Pacific Islands. . . . The morale of the people of Hawaii and Alaska, who are our fellow-citizens, will be heightened if we show them that we truly regard them as our equals in the responsibilities and privileges of statehood.

Letter to Vice President Barkley on Statehood
November 27

1951 Swings of the Pendulum

Under massive Chinese attack, the U.N. forces withdrew from the thirty-eighth parallel, and by January 4, the Communists occupied Seoul, the South Korean capital, for the second time. The Chinese offensive died out on January 24 along a front fifty miles south of Seoul due primarily to persistent air strikes at their tenuous supply lines. Lieutenant General Matthew Ridgway, commander of the Eighth Army, immediately launched a counteroffensive which, by late April, had carried the U.N. troops about twenty miles north of the thirty-eighth parallel. After a couple of more swings of the pendulum, on June 15 the battlefront lay more or less astride that parallel, where it remained as truce negotiations began on July 10.

President Truman relieved General MacArthur of his command on April 11, climaxing a long-smoldering dispute over extension of the war beyond the Yalu, which Truman opposed. The general had been making public statements on foreign policy in direct disobedience to orders from his commander in chief. After reviewing the case and the President's decision, General George C. Marshall, then Secretary of Defense, said: "The s.o.b. should have been fired two years ago."

But when MacArthur returned to the States, he received a hero's welcome, a glorifying ticker-tape parade in New York and an invitation to speak before Congress, where his sentimental closing phrase, "Old soldiers never die; they just fade away," caught the nation's fancy. Despite calls for his impeachment, the President, on firm Constitutional ground, never wavered. When it was later suggested that his had been a courageous act, Truman replied, "Courage has nothing to do with it. General MacArthur was insubordinate and I fired him. That's all there was to it."

The truce negotiations dragged on through 1951, while the President made it clear to the Communists that we would not give up the crucial high ground north of the thirty-eighth parallel which would be South Korea's best defense against another surprise attack. By 1952 only one point remained in dispute to prevent a truce: The Communists demanded that all 132,000 Chinese and North Korean prisoners be returned, but Truman said that the 60,000 who did not want to be returned to Communist territory would not be handed over. If the President had not held to this principle, he could have ended the war before the 1952 elections, to the immense political advantage of his party.

Meanwhile, he felt great admiration for the men fighting the frustrating war. He frequently told those men to whom he awarded the Medal of Honor, "I would rather wear this medal than be President of the United States."

After being pushed down the Korean Peninsula, the U.S. Eighth Army, commanded by General Matthew B. Ridgway *(opposite, at left)*, here with his Chief of Staff, General Rinaldo Van Brunt, bounced back to force the Communists north of the 38th parallel by April. That month Truman relieved General MacArthur of his Far East command, replacing him with Ridgway. Jacob Burch's cartoon *(below)* depicted the rage many people felt at MacArthur's dismissal.

Who does Truman think he is —— the PRESIDENT?"

Truce in Korea

. . . The free nations, however, are bound together by more than ideals. They are a real community bound together also by the ties of self-interest and self-preservation. . . .

The Soviet Union does not have to attack the United States to secure domination of the world. It can achieve its ends by isolating us and swallowing up our allies. . . . The best way to stop subversion by the Kremlin is to strike at the roots of social injustice and economic disorder. . . . The Soviet rulers have made it clear that we must have strength as well as right on our side. . . . Above all, we must remember that the fundamentals of our strength rest upon the freedoms of our people.

. . . When I request unity, what I am really asking for is a sense of responsibility on the part of every member of this Congress. Let us debate the issues, but let every man among us weigh his words and deeds. . . . Let each of us put our country ahead of our party, and ahead of our own personal interests. . . . This is our cause — peace, freedom, justice.

State of the Union Address
January 8

. . . I hope it will be remembered for its sincere effort for world peace, and if we accomplish that, if we get through this era without a third World War, I think that probably is what it will be remembered for. . . .

The administration of no President can be correctly evaluated during his term or within twenty-five or thirty years after that term. Thomas Jefferson has just now come into his own as a President.

Answer to Question of What He'd Like His Administration
To Be Remembered For
March 15

. . . In the simplest terms, what we are doing in Korea is this: We are trying to prevent a third World War. . . . The best time to meet the threat is in the beginning. It is easier to put out a fire in the beginning when it is small than after it has become a roaring blaze. . . .

If the Communist authorities realize they cannot defeat us in Korea, if they realize it would be foolhardy to widen the hostilities beyond Korea, then they may recognize the folly of continuing their aggression. A peaceful settlement may then be possible. The door is always open. . . .

Defeat of aggression in Korea may be the turning point in the world's search for a practical way of achieving peace and security.

Radio Address on Far Eastern Policy
April 11

With deep regret I have concluded that General of the Army Douglas MacArthur is unable to give his wholehearted support to the policies of the U.S. Government and of the U.N. in matters pertaining to his official duties. In view of the specific responsibilities imposed upon me by the Constitution [and] the added responsibility which has been entrusted to me by the U.N., I have decided that I must make a change of command in the Far East. . . .

Full and vigorous debate on matters of national policy is a vital element in the constitutional system of our free democracy. It is fundamental, however, that military commanders must be governed by the policies and directives issued to them in the manner provided by our laws and Constitution. . . .

General MacArthur's place in history as one of our greatest commanders is fully established. The nation owes him a debt of gratitude . . . I repeat my regret at the necessity for the action I feel compelled to take in this case.

Announcement of the Dismissal of MacArthur
April 11

. . . Some things have not changed at all since 1776. For one thing, freedom is still expensive. It still costs money. It still costs blood. It still calls for courage and endurance, not only in soldiers, but in every man and woman who is free and who is determined to remain free. . . . For another thing, the ideas on which our Government is founded — the ideas of equality, of God-given rights, of self-government — are still revolutionary.

. . . Men of the armed forces in Korea, you will go down in history as the first army to fight under the flag of a world organization in the defense of human freedom. You have fought well and without reproach. You have enslaved no free man, you have destroyed no free nation, you are guiltless of any country's blood. . . . You cannot transfix a lie with a bayonet, or blast deceit with machine-gun fire. The only weapons against such enemies are truth and fair dealing.

Independence Day Address
July 4

1951

Major General Lewis Pick accompanied
the Trumans on a firsthand look at the damage
caused by the devastating July floods in the
Missouri River Valley. Over 200,000 were left
homeless and 41 were killed.

If the government of the Soviet Union wants to make progress toward peace, it can stop flouting the authority of the United Nations, it can cease supporting armed aggression in defiance of the verdict of the United Nations, it can make constructive contributions toward establishing conditions of peace with Germany, Austria and Japan, . . . it can cease supporting subversive movements in other countries, it can cease its distortions of the motives and actions of other peoples and governments. . . .

Report to Congress on Continued Soviet Hostility
August 20

. . . It is a sobering thought that, but for the strength of this country and our willingness to use it if necessary, there might now be no human freedom in the world.

Message at Democratic National Committee Dinner, New York
November 26

Constitutional Freedoms

. . . Real Americanism means that we will protect freedom of speech. . . . Real Americanism means freedom of religion. . . . Real Americanism means fair opportunities for all our citizens. . . . Real Americanism means fair play. . . . Real Americanism means also that liberty is not license. There is no freedom to injure others. The Constitution does not protect free speech to the extent of permitting conspiracies to overthrow the Government. Neither does the right of free speech authorize slander or character assassination.

. . . Americanism needs defending — here and now. . . . It is being undermined by some people in this country who are loudly proclaiming that they are its chief defenders. . . . They

President Truman enjoyed some sightseeing during a trip to Hawaii *(above)*. Truman had taught himself to speak effectively without losing the unmistakable Missouri touch *(opposite)*. He preferred to speak "off the cuff" because his sincerity and natural dry wit were then more apparent.

90

are trying to create fear and suspicion among the people by the use of slander, unproved accusations, and just plain lies. . . . These slander mongers are trying to get us so hysterical that no one will stand up to them for fear of being called a Communist. . . . Character assassination is their stock in trade. Guilt by association is their motto. . . . It is not the American way to slur the loyalty and besmirch the character of the innocent and the guilty alike.

Address Dedicating Washington American
Legion Headquarters
August 14

. . . Although the nation has always united against any external peril, blind obedience to authority has never been characteristic of Americans. Rather, they have been questioners, doubters, experimenters, and very often articulate and vociferous dissenters. This attitude is perhaps our unique and most valuable national asset. . . . It has forced discussion, examination and re-examination of policies on every level.

Letter to Criminal Law Secretary of
National Bar Association
September 1

A constitution that is not adaptable — that prevents the government from acting for the general welfare of the people — will not long survive. . . . Ours is not such a constitution. We have discovered, over the years, that it offers the means for correcting present evils without throwing away past gains. . . . The wisdom of our form of government is that no men, no matter how good they appear to be, may be entrusted with absolute power.

The great achievement of government is that it has enabled us to meet the changing needs of the people while providing a rule of law that restrains all men, even the most powerful. The glory of our form of government lies in the fact that it has held us faithful to the concept that the aims of government are human betterment and human freedom.

Constitution Day Address
September 17

. . . Voluntary action by people who believe in a common cause is still the greatest force in the world. It is far more effective than any form of tyranny or despotism.

Radio Address to Open 1951 Red Cross Appeal
February 27

. . . We believe that there is something sacred about every human soul that God has put on this earth. . . . The average American baby born this year can expect to live 67 years — until the year 2018. And I was 67 last month. Too bad. . . .

What I want is a good workable plan that will enable all Americans to pay for the medical care they need. . . . Public health work is the key to improving conditions in the underdeveloped areas. No funds we spend will bring richer rewards in human progress and in strength for peace.

Speech at Dedication of National Institutes of Health
Clinical Center, Bethesda, Maryland
June 22

1952 McCarthyism and the Specter of Communists in Government

In 1952, Truman's final year in office, three inter-related items were paramount in his activities and concern: 1) To bow out of national politics while helping his party remain in power; 2) To bring the truce negotiations in Korea to a conclusion; 3) To denounce the demagogues, such as Senator Joseph McCarthy of Wisconsin, who, in the President's opinion, were riding the crest of the wave of anti-Communism for their own selfish ends, regardless of who was hurt and without concern for democratic principles.

He announced in March that he would not seek reelection, but he was unable to stem the tide that brought General Dwight Eisenhower to the White House. Among the reasons for this were that Truman was unable to bring about a Korean truce and the growing specter of Communists in Government.

President Truman was far from ignorant of the need for the Government to protect itself from Communist spies. In March 1947, he ordered an investigation into the loyalty of all employees of the Executive Branch. When this program was completed in April 1951, of the more than three million investigated, the vast majority were cleared; 3,000 resigned and 212 were dismissed. In August 1950, the President recommended legislation to remedy defects in the law, following the twin guidelines that "the United States shall be secure," and "equally . . . that we shall keep our historic liberties." But he vetoed the bill Congress passed (the McCarran Internal Security Act) which ignored his recommendations. He thought it would be ineffective against Communism and it violated "our own liberties." Congress overrode his veto.

The issue of Communists in Government first made the headlines during the summer of 1948 when Elizabeth Bentley and Whittaker Chambers told the House Un-American Activities Committee (H.U.A.C.) a startling tale of Communist espionage in the upper levels of the Federal Government. Among those that they accused was Alger Hiss, director of the Office of Political Affairs for the State Department. Truman called the charges "a red herring," raised by the Republicans to obscure their poor record in the Eightieth Congress. He said H.U.A.C. was the most "un-American activity in . . . Government." Hiss was convicted in January 1950 of perjury for denying he had passed secret documents to Communist spies. Later that year Senator McCarthy claimed there was large-scale Communist infiltration in the State Department, a charge a Senate committee found to be untrue. No evidence was produced by McCarthy and no convictions arose out of his charges. But the phenomenon of McCarthyism was well on its way to being one of the pervasive issues of the 1950's.

Meanwhile, in 1949, President Truman announced that the Russians had exploded an atomic bomb. When, within the next two years, it was revealed that its development had been facilitated by the espionage of Klaus Fuchs in Britain and Julius and Ethel Rosenberg in the United States, the emotional fervor of anti-Communist sentiment and McCarthyism increased. As the Republicans in 1952 increasingly applied the phrase "soft on Communism" to the Democrats and the Truman Administration, the President struck back, accusing McCarthy of using the "big lie" and of being a "character assassin." He attacked the Republican candidate, General Eisenhower, for not having denounced McCarthy's calling Eisenhower's former mentor, General George C. Marshall, a "front for traitors" and for supporting McCarthy for re-election. After Truman left office, McCarthy implied that even he was a traitor and subpoenaed him to appear at a Congressional investigation. The former President refused.

McCarthyism ran rampant toward the end of Truman's term in office. A continuous string of Government officials were called to hearings *(opposite)* where they were questioned by Senator Joseph McCarthy *(at left)*. The Wisconsin senator *(below)* never let up on his accusations of Communist infiltration.

Good Government

Q. Mr. President, this week Senator McCarthy attacked Philleo Nash on your staff, and said he had F.B.I. reports, and I want to know if you had any comment on that, or intend to ask Mr. Hoover how that could be possible?

The President. It's in the same line as all the attacks that the pathological Mr. McCarthy has made on all of the Government employees that he doesn't like.

Q. Do you think he is telling the truth when he says he bases that speech on F.B.I. reports?

The President. Does he ever tell the truth? If he does, I haven't found it out.

Q. A couple of weeks ago he attacked Mr. Lloyd, also on your staff, and he said at that time he had received some information from the Loyalty Review Board. Do you think — is that subject being investigated?

The President. I doubt very much whether he received any information. He doesn't need information to become a character assassin. That's his business. And I'm not talking with immunity.

[McCarthy had said that Nash had joined the Communist Party in "early 1940's" and had been a "close associate" of members of a Canadian Red spy ring. Nash replied that McCarthy had told a "contemptible lie."]

Presidential News Conference
January 31

. . . Let me tell you something I have learned in my thirty years of public office: Good government is good politics; and the best politics is what is best for all the people. . . . There is no room in Government service for anyone who is not true to his public trust. . . . I'm starting now and I'm giving warning to the people who've been slandering the Government employees that they're going to have trouble with me from now until November. And the best part of it is I'm not running for anything.

Civil Service League Speech
May 2

Then there is Bill Benton [Senator from Conn.]. Bill is always on the right side of every tough fight that comes along. And the thing I admire about him most is his courage. He has stepped right up and tagged Joe McCarthy for what he is, when a lot of other people were running for cover — or were even doing a little sordid coattail riding. [Benton had accused McCarthy of using "Hitlerlike" tactics in his anti-Communist campaign and offered to waive his Congressional immunity to let McCarthy sue.]

Address at Keel Laying of U.S.S. *Nautilus*, Groton, Conn.
June 14

. . . As your President, I have to think about the effects that a steel shutdown here would have all over the world. . . . I would not be faithful to my responsibilities as President if I did not use every effort to help this from happening. With American troops facing the enemy on the field of battle, I would not be living up to my oath of office if I failed to do whatever is required to provide them with the weapons and the ammunition they need for their survival.

Therefore, I am taking two actions tonight. First, I am directing the Secretary of Commerce to take possession of the steel mills, and to keep them operating. Second, I am directing the Acting Director of Defense Mobilization to get the representatives of the steel companies down here to Washington at the earliest possible date in renewed effort to get them to settle their dispute. . . . I don't want to see the Government running the steel plants a minute longer than is absolutely necessary to prevent a shutdown.

On Federal Seizure of the Steel Industry
April 8

. . . Local self-government is both the right and responsibility of free men. The denial of self-government does not benefit the National Capital of the world's largest and most powerful democracy.

Not only is the lack of self-government an injustice to the people of the District of Columbia, but it imposes a needless burden on the Congress and it tends to convert the principles for which this country stands before the world.

On Self-Government for Washington, D.C.
May 1

The greatest vice of the present quota system, however, is that it discriminates, deliberately and intentionally, against many of the peoples of the world. The purpose behind it was to cut down and virtually eliminate immigration to this

1952

President Truman initialed the keel of the first nuclear submarine, the U.S.S. *Nautilus (opposite)*, at Groton, Connecticut, on June 14. A week earlier he had awarded the Distinguished Service Medal to General Dwight D. Eisenhower, with Mamie Eisenhower in attendance. Soon after, "Ike" retired from the army to begin his Presidential election campaign.

country from southern and eastern Europe. A theory was invented to rationalize this objective. The theory was that in order to be readily assimilable, European immigrants should be admitted in proportion to the numbers of persons of their respective national stocks already here as shown by the census of 1920. Since Americans of English, Irish, and German descent were most numerous, immigrants of those three nationalities got the lion's share — more than two-thirds — of the quota. The remaining third was divided up among all the other nations given quotas. . . .

The idea behind this discriminatory policy was, to put it baldly, that Americans with English or Irish names were better people and better citizens than Americans with Italian or Greek or Polish names. . . . It violates the great political doctrine of the Declaration of Independence that "all men are created equal." It denies the humanitarian creed inscribed beneath the Statue of Liberty proclaiming to all nations, "Give me your tired, your poor, your huddled masses yearning to breathe free."

It repudiates our basic religious concepts, our belief in the brotherhood of man, and in the words of St. Paul that "there is neither Jew nor Greek, there is neither bond nor free, . . . for ye are all one in Christ Jesus."

The basis of this quota system was false and unworthy in 1924. It is even worse now.

Veto of McCarran-Walter Immigration Act in
Message to Congress
June 25

Struggle for Peace

. . . We have a great responsibility to conduct our political fights in a manner that does not harm the national interest. We can find plenty of things to differ about without destroying our free institutions and without abandoning our bipartisan foreign policy. . . . This is a time for courage, not for grumbling and mumbling.

. . . My friends of the Congress, less than one-third of the expenditure of the cost of World War II should have created the developments necessary to feed the whole world so we would not have to fight against stomach Communism. . . .

This Government of ours — the Congress and the Executive both — must keep working to bring about a fair deal for all the American people. . . . This demonstration of the way free men govern themselves has a more powerful influence on the people of the world — on both sides of the Iron Curtain — than all the trick slogans and pie-in-the-sky promises of the Communists.

Some say that we should give up the struggle for peace, and others say we should have a war and get it over with. That's a terrible statement, though I've heard it made. . . . Let us prove again that we are not merely sunshine patriots and summer soldiers. Let us go forward, trusting in the God of Peace, to win the goals we seek.

State of the Union Address
January 9

. . . The Soviet policy is the old one: Divide and conquer. Our policy is an old one, too: In unity there is strength. . . . I challenge anyone to tell me how this country is going to defend itself if we abandon our allies and hold up on this continent. It is perfectly plain that it cannot be done.

. . . We know the Communist promises are false, but it would be ridiculous to go to the peoples of Asia and Africa and the Near East and say, "Here are guns to drive away the men who are promising you what you have always wanted." Stomach Communism cannot be halted with weapons of war. . . . This is not a program to carry the world on our shoulders. It is a program to make it possible for the world to stand on its own feet.

Appeal to the Nation for Foreign Aid (Mutual
Security Program)
March 6

. . . There is nothing of imperialism in our concept of Point Four. We do not propose to dominate other people, or exploit them, or force them to change their ways of life.

. . . The two ideas that guide Point Four are, first, cooperation, freely sought, and, second, help to those who want to help themselves. . . .

Address on Point-Four Program
April 8

Democratic Campaign

My favorite animal is the mule. He has a lot more horse sense than a horse. He knows when to stop eating. And he knows when to stop working.

January

1952

Truman had privately supported Adlai Stevenson as his successor for months, but the Illinois governor had refused to accept formal candidacy until a confused Democratic Convention drafted him in Chicago on July 26. Truman applauded Stevenson *(opposite)* after he received the nomination. As a result of the hard-fought campaign, the Republicans captured the Presidency for the first time since 1928. Truman rode with President-elect Eisenhower *(below)* on their way to the Capitol for inauguration proceedings in January 1953.

. . . I shall not be a candidate for reelection. I have served my country long and, I think, efficiently and honestly. I shall not accept a renomination. I do not feel that it is my duty to spend another four years in the White House.

Jefferson-Jackson Day Dinner Address
March 29

[You have] nominated a winner. . . . [I will] take off my coat and go out and help him win.

Presenting Presidential Nominee Adlai Stevenson
to the Democratic Convention
July 26

. . . My grandfather used to tell me that whenever you see a fellow go up to the mourner's bench in a Baptist church and begin to pray out loud, you'd better go home and lock your smokehouse.

. . . Surely the Republican candidate must know the Iron Curtain and the Kremlin walls will not come tumbling down from a few blasts on a campaign trumpet.

Speech at Parkersburg, West Virginia
September 2

Some of the generals and the admirals and the career men in Government look upon the occupant of the White House as only a temporary nuisance who soon will be succeeded by another temporary occupant who won't find out what it is all about for a long time and then it will be too late to do anything about it.

The Republicans have General Motors and General Electric and General Foods and General MacArthur and General Martin and General Wedemeyer. And they have their own five-star general running for President. . . . I want to say to you that every general I know is on this list except general welfare, and general welfare is in with the corporals and privates in the Democratic Party.

General Marshall is the finest example of a patriotic American. He was the organizer of our army, the architect of victory in World War II, a self-sacrificing, tireless public official. He needs no praise from me. He is the standard by which we judge the patriotism and loyalty of other men.

This great man has been the subject of an infamous attack by two Republican isolationist senators [McCarthy and William Jenner of Indiana]. Acting from purely partisan motives, these two moral pigmies have called this great American a "living lie," a "front for traitors" and the center of an infamous conspiracy. Nothing more contemptible has ever occurred in the long history of human spite and envy. It is unspeakable, and the authors of these slanders are unworthy of the company of decent men and women.

Now what has the Republican candidate [General Eisenhower] done about this outrage? Has he condemned these two slanderers? Has he denounced their lies about his great friend and benefactor?

I'll tell you what he has done. He has endorsed them both for reelection to the Senate. One he has embraced publicly. The other he has humbly thanked for riding on his campaign train.

Address at Colorado Springs
October 7

I like Ike — I like Ike so well I would send him back to the army if I had a chance.

October 12

. . . A Presidential election, my friends, is more than a popularity contest. It is a serious business — it is a serious business in which a nation decides its course. It is an act by which we give one man power over the future of all of us. We must have a President we can trust.

Speech at Pittsburgh
October 22

Views of the Presidency

I have tried my best to give the nation everything I had in me. There are a great many people, probably a million people, who could have done the job better than I did, but I had the job and I had to do it and I always quote an epitaph on a tombstone in a cemetery in Tombstone, Arizona: "Here lies Jack Williams. He done his damnedest." I think that is the greatest epitaph a man can have.

300th Press Conference
April 17

. . . I am sometimes accused of claiming credit for every good thing that has happened in the United States while I have been President, and, by the same token, accused of never admitting a mistake.

As for the mistakes, I know that I make them like everybody else does, and I do admit them from time to time. However, it has not seemed necessary for me to spend a great deal of time calling attention to my mistakes because there have always been plenty of other people who were willing to do that for me.

Speech to American Hospital Association
September 16

The greatest part of the President's job is to make decisions — big ones and small ones, dozens of them almost every day. The papers may circulate around the Government for awhile but they finally reach this desk. And then there's no place else for them to go. The President — whoever he is — has to decide. He can't pass the buck to anybody. . . .

I suppose that history will remember my term in office as the years when the "cold war" began to overshadow our lives. I have had hardly a day in office that has not been dominated by this all-embracing struggle. . . . And always in the background there has been the atomic bomb. But when history says that my term of office saw the beginning of the "cold war," it will also say that in those eight years we have set the course that can win it.

It was not easy to make the decision that sent American boys again into battle. I was a soldier in the first World War

1952

The Truman family greeted throngs of well-wishers from their car's rear platform at Union Station in Washington after Eisenhower's inauguration. The former President, beginning his return to private life in Independence, was grateful and pleased at the enthusiastic send-off given to "plain Mr. Truman."

and I know what a soldier goes through. I knew well the anguish that mothers and fathers and families go through. So I knew what was ahead if we acted in Korea. But after all this was said we realized that the issue was whether there would be fighting in a limited area now or on a much larger scale later on — whether there would be some casualties now or many more casualties later. So a decision was reached — the decision I believe was the most important in my time as President. In the days that followed, the most heartening fact was that the American people clearly agreed with the decision.

. . . So, as I empty the drawers of this desk, and as Mrs. Truman and I leave the White House, we have no regret. We feel we have done our best in the public service. I hope and believe we have contributed to the welfare of this nation and to the peace of the world.

Farewell as President
January 15, 1953

Courage and Humility

The personality of Harry S. Truman was made up of a remarkable combination of qualities — self-confidence and humility, steadfastness and flexibility, honesty and political shrewdness, courage and a willingness to compromise, simplicity and profundity, frankness and kindness. But of all of these, courage and humility were perhaps the most pervasive ones.

Harry Truman often said he had received his education in the army, and it was here that his courage first revealed itself, although it was not in combat, as such, but in terms of leadership that this

quality came forth. When Captain Truman took over Battery "D" in France during World War I, its men were known for their rowdiness and lack of discipline. "When I first took command," he recalled years later, "I called all the sergeants and corporals together. I told them I knew they had been making trouble for the previous commanders. I said, 'I didn't come over here to get along with you. You've got to get along with me. And if there are any who can't, speak up and I'll bust you right back.' We got along."

The humility of Harry Truman was little apparent to the general public, including many who supported him enthusiastically. His essential humility and lack of pretentiousness were shown, for example, in his attitude toward the servants while he was in the White House. As his daughter tells it in her book, *Harry S. Truman:*

Dad was never particularly happy being waited on by the numerous servants in the White House. It offended his ingrained Missouri sense of equality.

The White House staff was astonished, for instance, when Dad introduced his brother Vivian to Alonzo Fields, the head butler, and they shook hands before Vivian sat down at the table. . . . Whenever a new man went on duty in the dining room, Fields introduced him. Dad would stand up, shake hands with him, and say, "Now don't be disturbed by me. . . ."

His deep-seated humility was also displayed when he said in 1959, "I wasn't one of the great Presidents, but I had a good time trying to be one." The verdict of a later generation is going against him on this opinion.

Truman's relationships with his self-effacing wife and his sprightly, intelligent daughter were unusually close, genuinely warm and constantly enlivened with humor. During the 1948 campaign, at the end of his speeches from the rear platform of the "Truman Special," he frequently would introduce Mrs. Truman with "I want you to meet the boss," followed by, "and here's the one who bosses her," as daughter Margaret came into view. But Mr. Truman could be agonizingly serious about them. After he wrote a scurrulous letter in 1950 to the music critic who had criticized Margaret's singing, Truman expected the attacks by the press but was annoyed by aides who thought his note was a mistake because it damaged his image as President. He told them that the public would be on his side and predicted that his mail would be eighty percent in favor of his action, and his prediction proved correct. Many mothers said they would have wanted their husbands to defend their daughters as he had done. He told his staff that they didn't understand human nature.

The French gave Truman an enthusiastic welcome on his visit to Paris *(opposite)* in May 1956. Sprightly and intelligent, his daughter Margaret appeared on television and radio shows, here with Fred Allen *(below)*.

. . . I have always considered my mother and father as my first great influence. I was lucky to have picked the right mother and father. . . .

Address to Mid-Century White House Conference
on Children and Youth
December 5, 1950

You know, I went to Sunday school right across there — the first time in my life, a long, long time ago and in that Sunday school class I met a little, blue-eyed, golden-haired girl — my first sweetheart. Her eyes are still blue, but her hair is no longer golden; it's silver — like mine. And she is still my sweetheart.

Speaking of Mrs. Truman
November 6, 1950

. . . I always give my occupation as "farmer." I spent the best ten years of my life trying to run a 600-acre farm successfully, and I know what the problems are.

Remark to Delegation from Ohio Farm Bureau Federation
May 24, 1950

I can't let Jim Wadsworth have you believe that he is the only farmer in the place. I am one, too. And there are a great many people who would tell you that that is still where I belong.

Address to Representatives of Management and Labor, Philadelphia
November 19, 1943

. . . I think I have told you before that the happiest ten years of my life were spent on the floor of the Senate. I used to sit in this seat, and I had a seat here for the simple reason that when the going was too rough, there was always a way to get out. [In reference to his seat being within ten feet of the door.]

Speech on Visit to the Senate
June 24, 1953

I heard a fellow tell a story about how he felt when he had to make speeches. He said when he has to make a speech, he felt like the fellow who was at the funeral of his wife, and the undertaker had asked him if he would ride down to the cemetery in the same car with his mother-in-law. He said, "Well, I can do it, but it's just going to spoil the whole day for me."

September 18, 1948

. . . I heard a story one time about a fellow who thought he was very good. He said he could lick anybody in the county. Then he said he could lick anybody in the state. Finally, he said he could lick anybody in the world, and that is when he got whipped in a minute. I hope that doesn't happen to me.

Upon Introduction in Washington to Handicapped
Children as "Greatest Guy in the World"
June 21, 1950

Miss Truman: I am frequently asked what kind of work — manual work, that is — you do around the house.
Mr. Truman: I do an immense amount of it from a rocking chair.

Margaret Interviews her Father on "Person to Person" TV Program
May 27, 1955

Had dinner by myself tonight. Work in Lee House office until dinnertime. A butler came in very formally and said, "Mr. President, dinner is served." I walked into the dining room in the Blair House. Barnett in tails and white tie pulls out my chair, pushes me up to the table. John in tails and white tie brings me a fruit cup, Barnett takes away the empty cup. John brings me a plate, Barnett brings me carrots and beets. I have to eat alone and in silence in candlelit room. I ring. Barnett takes the plate and butter plates. John comes in with a napkin and silver crumb tray — there are no crumbs but John has to brush them off the table anyway. Barnett brings me a plate with a finger bowl and doily on it. I remove the finger bowl and doily and John puts a glass saucer and a little bowl on the plate. Barnett brings me some chocolate custard. John brings me a demitasse (at home a little cup of coffee — about two good gulps) and my dinner is over. I take a hand bath in the finger bowl and go back to work. What a life!

Humorous Note on Dining by Himself at White House
November 1, 1949

. . . Mr. Cannon, in introducing me, made the statement that he was introducing the most powerful man in the world, who is now President of the United States. And I explained to the Congressman that I didn't think that was quite true because I couldn't get my wife and daughter up to come with me.

Extemporaneous Remarks to Women's Division,
Democratic National Committee
January 21, 1949

102

Margaret Truman teamed with Jimmy Durante and Eddie Jackson *(above)* for a television show in the early 1950's. During the 1956 Democratic Convention, Truman, still active in politics, appeared on the rostrum *(opposite)* with Vice Presidential nominee Estes Kefauver, Presidential nominee Adlai Stevenson, and Senate leader Lyndon Johnson.

I do not like to hunt animals, and I never have. I do not believe in shooting at anything that cannot shoot back.

Comment on Hunting
1960

. . . I appreciate this more than any meeting I have ever attended as President or Vice President or Senator. This is the greatest demonstration that any man could have, because I'm just Mr. Truman, private citizen now.

This is the first time you have ever sent me home in a blaze of glory. I can't adequately express my appreciation for what you are doing. I'll never forget it if I live to be a hundred.

And that's just what I expect to do!

Delivered from rear platform of train at Union Station, Washington, D.C.,
to crowd giving Truman family send-off on their return to Independence
January 20, 1953

I have just read your lousy review. . . . It seems to me that you are a frustrated old man* that never made a success, an eight-ulcer man on a four-ulcer job and all four ulcers working. I never met you but if I do you'll need a new nose and plenty of beefsteak and perhaps a supporter below.

Note in longhand to Paul Hume, Washington Post music critic
(After reading Hume's review of concert by daughter Margaret)
December 6, 1950

*Hume was 34. He opened his next recital review: "If I may venture to express an opinion . . ."

Epilogue

One of the strengths of Harry Truman during the years he was a Senator and President in Washington, D.C., was that he really never left Independence, Missouri. So after General Eisenhower was inaugurated President on January 20, 1953, the Trumans immediately headed home to the white clapboard house in Independence. A huge throng gave the Truman family a warm send-off at Washington's Union Station. Another 10,000 greeted them enthusiastically at the railroad station when they arrived at home.

The former President's attention during the years following his return to Independence was concentrated on putting his papers in order so that he could write his *Memoirs* and on planning the Harry S. Truman Library which opened in 1957. In 1956, Mr. and Mrs. Truman went to England where they visited Winston Churchill and the former President received a degree from Oxford. He campaigned vigorously in 1956 for Adlai Stevenson in a losing cause and in 1957 he became a grandfather. The Trumans accepted an invitation from President John F. Kennedy in 1961 to have dinner at the White House, where the former President played the piano. In 1965, President Lyndon B. Johnson flew to Independence to sign the Medicare bill into law at the Truman Library because the former President had begun the struggle for such a bill twenty years before.

But more significant and certainly surprising to many Americans, especially those critical of Harry Truman while he was President, the man from Independence began to enter a realm of the national consciousness usually reserved for military and sports heroes and very few politicians: He became part of America's mythology. As pretentious and devious men began to dominate American government and as they were revealed to the people during the 1960's and '70's, Harry Truman joined his long-time idol, Andrew Jackson, to become a true folk hero. So that when, in 1975, thirty years after Truman became President, a winning Senatorial candidate was asked on national television what kind of Democrat he was, he replied proudly, "I'm a Harry Truman Democrat."

Although no longer President, Truman *(opposite)* did not remain inactive as a private citizen. His instinctive urge to meet ordinary citizens caused his popularity to grow. Here, he met an engineer *(below)* of the train returning him to Missouri in 1953.

Presidential Remembrances

I was one of those persons who hardly ever got the job he wanted in politics but who, when he got it, gave it everything he had. I've tried my best to do my best in every political office I ever had. I think thirty years' service is enough, and I am just as happy as I can be, trying to be a private citizen, and it's a hell of a job.

> Speech to National Press Club
> May 10, 1954

. . . If we [Truman and General Marshall] are traitors, the country is in a hell of a fix. I have served my country for thirty years in military and civilian capacities and to be called a traitor by a Vice President of the United States is hard to take. It is an awful thing to be called a traitor.

> Remarks on Richard Nixon Calling Him a Traitor in 1954
> February 3, 1956

I'll never forgive Nixon for calling me a traitor.

> News Conference, Syracuse, New York
> April 23, 1960

. . . It makes me proud when somebody calls me a politician. A politician is a man who understands government, and who knows how to make it run. And when a man is a politician, after he has been dead about 50 years they'll label him a statesman. I have no desire — at this time — to be a statesman.

> Remarks at Benjamin Franklin Awards Dinner, New York
> Employing Printers Association
> January 14, 1958

. . . I'm going to run again when I'm 90. You know, the last time I said that, some damn fool looked it up and found that when I'm 90 it's an off year and I can't run anyway.

> Lecture at Columbia University
> April 28, 1959

Politics and the Presidency

. . . No office ever had the powers or responsibilities of the Presidency, and you'll never hear me criticizing it. I may differ with policy, but I won't attack the office. No man can fill it in an ideal manner.

> Remarks at Luncheon of Radio and Television Executive Society
> January 11, 1954

. . . When I was at the White House I used to keep on my desk a sign which said, "The buck stops here." That is a precept every President ought to have on his desk. And what is more, he ought to meet it.

> Talk to Indiana Democratic Editorial Association,
> French Lick, Indiana
> August 27, 1955

. . . No man, if he knows what it is all about, would want to be President. It is the most terrible job in the world as well as the most honorable. No, I don't want to be back in the White House. Sometimes I wish I was there to make decisions — but I'm not, so that's that. . . . If they are going

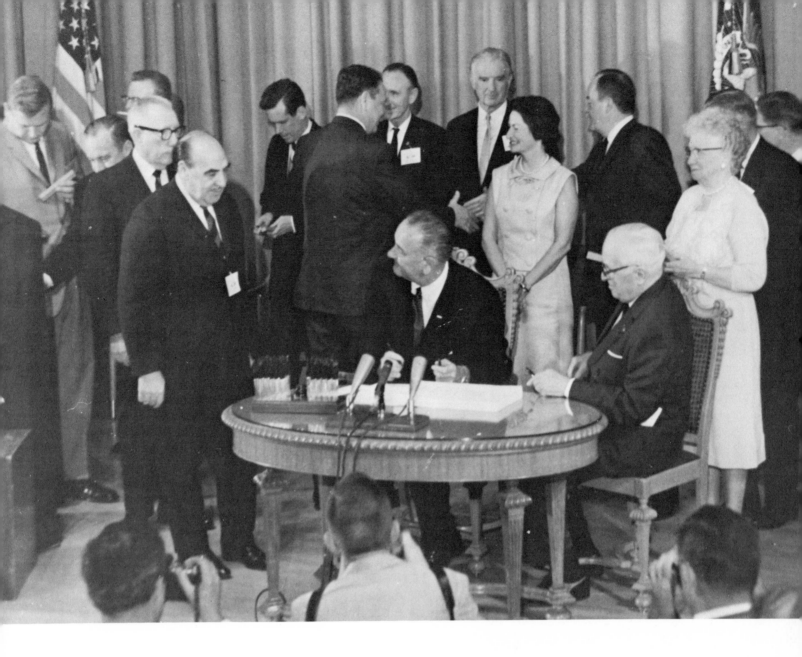

to have socialism by the time that little child [his new grand-
son] grows up to live under it, at least they are going to say
this: If I live these next three and a half years, the first three
and a half years are going to be a terrible battle.

Television Interview in Independence, Missouri
July 7, 1957

This library will belong to the people of the United States.
My papers will be the property of the people and be accessible
to them. And this is as it should be. The papers of the Presidents are among the most valuable sources of material for
history. They ought to be preserved and they ought to be used.

Speech at Truman Library Dedication
September 16, 1957

The happiest day I ever spent in my life was the day I left
the White House. They tried to kick me out, but they didn't
succeed in 1948, and if they hadn't done that I might have
quit then, but then whenever anybody tries to run over me
he finds out he's got something to run over, and that's all
there is to it.

Address at Hoover Library Dedication, West Branch, Iowa
August 10, 1962

Party Politics

. . . It behooves the American people, I think, to give Mr. Eisenhower a Democratic Congress and hope we can save him from the misdeeds of his own party.

Letter to Democratic National Committee
September 17, 1954

. . . The G.O.P. is just like the old Bourbons of France — they never learn anything and they never forget anything.

Speech at Des Moines, Iowa
April 11, 1956

Truman: Well, we're going to lick the hell out of the Republicans.
Announcer: I guess the ex-President of the United States is the only man who can get away with that word on radio.

Radio Comment
August 16, 1956

. . . I had my picture taken with several of the Republican leaders and several of the Democratic leaders. If that doesn't ruin them politically, they're bum proof. . . .

Speech at Bipartisan Meeting on Foreign Aid, Washington
February 25, 1958

. . . When a leader is in the Democratic party he's a boss; when he's in the Republican party he's a leader.

Lecture at Columbia University
April 28, 1959

. . . The damn farmers vote Republican. They ought to have their heads examined. They ought to have more than that — they ought to lose everything they've got if they do it again. . . .

I wish I had time to tell you all the things that you are for — that Democrats are for — that Nixon has voted against. And that bird has the nerve to come to Texas and ask you to vote for him. . . . If you vote for Nixon, you ought to go to hell.

Speech at Fund-Raising Dinner, San Antonio
October 11, 1960

Still Working for Peace

. . . This is an important hour for the nation. For those of our citizens who have completed their tour of duty and have moved to the sidelines, these are the days that we are trying to celebrate for them. These people are our prideful responsibility and they are entitled, among other benefits, to the best medical protection available.

Remarks at Signing of Medicare Bill at Truman Library
July 30, 1965

. . . My friends, this is the first time in more than 30 years that I have not been in public office. I'm out of a job, and I'm having a wonderful time at it. But I'm still busy. I am only working eight hours a day now instead of sixteen. . . .

Because Truman had begun the struggle for a national health policy during his Presidential years, President Lyndon Johnson flew to Independence to sign the Medicare bill *(opposite)* on July 30, 1965. In 1957 Truman testified before a Congressional subcommittee *(below)* investigating the possibility of photocopying Presidential papers.

One of the advantages of being in so-called political retirement is that it gives a man more time to think. I have been thinking a lot, in recent months, of the path this country has followed in the past twenty years and of where it is heading.

. . . You can't hope to change the philosophy of those people who are now in Washington, but if you watch them closely and raise your voices loud and clear, you may be able to salvage some of these things [public welfare, low interest rates, etc.] After all, they are just politicians, and they are influenced by public opinion. So, I urge you to put up a good fight, day in and day out, for the things you believe in. . . .

My friends, we can't just turn away from the international situation and wish it didn't exist. . . . The world picture is full of hope today, just as it is full of danger. . . . We must negotiate with strength, my friends. Strength is what Communists understand and respect. Strength comes from unity with our allies, from the sympathetic understanding of all free peoples and from the power of our defense forces. . . . In our hopes for world peace and freedom we are not Republicans and Democrats; we are all Americans.

Address at Detroit Labor Rally
September 7, 1953

. . . War is fruitless, senseless and a tragic adventure. There are no victors, only victims. . . . Reviving ancient hostilities, enmities and prejudices will serve no useful purpose and will solve no outstanding problems. . . . War is a disease and should be treated as such.

Message of Founder of Harry S. Truman Center
for the Advancement of Peace, Los Angeles
January 18, 1967

Four Freedoms . . .

. . . The good life is not possible without freedom. It is not possible without freedom of inquiry and freedom of thought. It is not possible without freedom of worship and of the individual conscience before God. It is not possible without freedom from fear — fear of oppression that may come from a foreign foe or from a domestic source. And, lastly, the good life is not possible without the assurance of good health and daily bread for everyone. . . .

The responsibility for these freedoms falls on free men. And free men preserve them only if they are militant about freedom, only if they are willing to fight for it. We ought to get angry when these rights are violated, and make ourselves heard until the wrong is righted.

. . . Effective efforts to preserve freedom may involve discomfort and risk. It takes faith, unselfishness and courage to stand up to a bully, or to stand up for a whole community when it has been frightened into subjection. But it has to be done, if we are to remain free. . . .

Someone once said, "We die of what we eat and drink, but more, we die of what we think." Let us think — and act — as free men, and we shall live as a free nation and a free world.

Remarks on Acceptance of Four Freedoms Award
September 28, 1953

McCarthyism: the meaning of the word is the corruption of truth, the abandonment of our historical devotion to fair play. It is the abandonment of "due process" of law. It is the use of the big lie and the unfounded accusation against any citizen in the name of Americanism and security. It is the rise to power of the demagogue who lives on untruth; it is the spread of fear and the destruction of faith in every level of our society. . . . This horrible cancer is eating at the vitals of America and it can destroy the great edifice of freedom.

November 17, 1953

You must watch out for these people. But stand fast. In your time you'll have a demagogue or two. . . . The best way to handle a demagogoe is by ridicule: If you stick a pin in a stuffed shirt and let the air out, you know he's through.

Comments on the Ku Klux Klan and McCarthyism
April 29, 1959

. . . I am shocked beyond words at the tragedy that has happened to our country and to President Kennedy's family today. The President's death is a great personal loss to the country and to me. He was an able President, one the people loved and trusted.

Statement on J.F.K. Assassination
November 22, 1963

Truman, here walking with his grandson Clifton *(opposite)*, thoroughly enjoyed private life after nearly three decades of public service. In November 1961, the former President played the piano in the White House *(below)* at a dinner given in his honor by President and Mrs. John F. Kennedy.

Chronology

1884

May 8 — **Born** in Lamar, Mo., to John and Martha Ellen (Young) Truman

1890

Dec. 28 — Truman family moves to **Independence**, Mo.

1901

Graduates from **high school**

1917

Aug. — Mobilized with his **National Guard** regiment as a lieutenant

1918

March — **Sails** from New York **to France** in artillery of 35th Division

Sept.– Nov. — **Capt. Truman's battery** engaged in fighting at St.-Mihiel, on Meuse-Argonne front, before Verdun and at Metz

1919

May 6 — **Discharged** from army with rank of major

June 28 — **Marries** Elizabeth Virginia (Bess) Wallace in Independence, Mo.

Fall — With Eddie Jacobson, **opens haberdashery** in Kansas City

1922

Haberdashery fails; on Nov. 7, Truman **elected** Jackson County judge (non-judicial)

1924

Feb. 17 — **Daughter** Mary Margaret born

Nov. 4 — **Defeated** for reelection

1926

Nov. 2 — **Elected chief judge** of Jackson County

1934

Nov. 6 — Elected to U.S. **Senate**

1940

Nov. 5 — **Reelected** to U.S. Senate

1941–1944

Heads Special Committee to Investigate National Defense Program, which becomes known as the **"Truman Committee"**

1944

July 21 — Nominated candidate for **Vice President** on ticket with F.D.R. by Democratic National Convention with second ballot victory over incumbent Vice President Henry A. Wallace

Nov. 7 — Roosevelt–Truman **ticket wins election**

1945

April 12 — **Sworn in as President** in Cabinet Room of White House after death of F.D.R.

April 25 — President's telephoned speech opens **San Francisco Conference** establishing the United Nations Organization; briefed for first time on atomic bomb by Sec. of War Stimson

May 7 — Germany surrenders; **V–E Day** proclaimed next day

June 26 — President witnesses signing of **U.N. charter** in San Francisco

July 16 — **First atomic bomb** exploded in desert near Alamogordo, N.M.

July 17– Aug. 2 — President attends conference in **Potsdam**, Germany, with Churchill and Stalin

Aug. 6 — U.S. drops atomic bomb on **Hiroshima**, Japan (Aug. 5, U.S. time)

Aug. 8 — President **signs U.N. charter**

Aug. 14 — **Japan surrenders**; formal surrender aboard U.S.S. Missouri on Sept. 2 (Far Eastern time)

Sept. 4 — President calls Congress back into session and gives one of longest Presidential messages containing basic **Fair Deal** program (although term not used): basic social and economic reforms with Federal control of unemployment compensation, increase of minimum wage, a vast housing program and sweeping reorganization of executive branch

Nov. 19 — President proposes **Federal health insurance**, first President to do so

1946

Jan. 10 — First General Assembly of **United Nations** opens in London

Jan. 21 — President recommends **statehood** for Alaska and Hawaii in message to Congress

March 5 — Winston Churchill delivers **"Iron Curtain"** speech at Westminster College, Fulton, Mo.

June 29 — President vetoes bill extending Office of Price Administration's (**O.P.A.**) authority to control prices because of crippling amendments, thus he fails in his attempt to "hold the line" against inflation

July 4 — **Philippines'** independence granted by U.S.

July 26 — President wins enactment of **Atomic Energy Act** putting atomic power under civilian rather than military control

July 30 — Attorney General Tom Clark reports that the President has ordered Justice Dept. to probe **lynchings** of four Negroes in Georgia

Sept. 20 — President asks for and receives from **Henry A. Wallace** his resignation as Sec. of Commerce because of Wallace's public disagreement with anti-Soviet direction of the Administration's foreign policy

Sept. 30 — Twenty-two Nazi leaders convicted in **Nuremberg**, Ger., of war crimes by International Tribunal

Nov. 5 — Congressional **elections give Republicans sizable majorities** in both houses; President later calls it the "Do-Nothing" Congress

Dec. 4 — Federal judge **fines United Mine Workers** $3,510,000 and U.M.W. chief John L. Lewis $10,000 for criminal contempt of court

Dec. 31 — President proclaims **cessation of hostilities** of World War II

1947

March — President orders **investigation into loyalty** of all employees of Executive Branch. (Program continues until April 1951; 3,000 resign, 212 dismissed out of three million investigated)

March 12 — President asks Congress to appropriate $400 million for economic and military aid to Greece and Turkey; approved three days later. Beginning of **Truman Doctrine** for containment of Soviet imperialism

June 23 — **Taft–Hartley** Labor–Management Relations Act passed over President's veto

June 25 — Sec. of State George C. Marshall proposes in a speech at Harvard U. that U.S. extend financial aid to European nations to help in their recovery from war; proposal becomes known as **Marshall Plan**

July 26 — Congress approves **unification of armed services** under a Secretary of Defense

July 27 — President's **mother** dies in Grandview, Mo., at age 84

Aug. 15 — **India and Pakistan** gain **independence** from England

Sept. 29 — President appoints ex-President Herbert Hoover as chairman of 12-man board which will work on simplification and economy in Federal Government. Board becomes known as the **Hoover Commission**. (Commission reports in Feb.–March 1949 led to Reorganization Act of same year and later legislation.)

1948

Feb. 2 — President sends civil rights message to Congress, the most sweeping of its kind until this time. It proposes establishment of permanent commissions on **Federal Civil Rights** and **Fair Employment Practices** and the outlawing of "Jim Crow" in schools, transportation and public service facilities

Feb. 25 — **Coup d'etat** gives Communists control of Czechoslovakia

April 30 — Charter of Organization of American States (**O.A.S.**) signed at Bogota, Colombia

May 14 — State of **Israel proclaimed**; first de facto recognition comes from U.S.

June 11 — **Vandenberg Resolution** passed by Senate approves U.S. participation in regional security agreements

June 24 — Soviet military government in occupied Germany begins land blockade of Berlin's Allied sectors; beginning of 321-day **Berlin airlift** by Western powers

July — President issues Executive Order **prohibiting racial discrimination** in armed services

July 15 — President **nominated for reelection** by Democrats; Sen. Alben Barkley nominated as Vice Presidential candidate

July 30 — **Elizabeth Bentley** makes first public accusations about Communist spies in upper levels of Federal Government

Nov. 2	President **reelected** in closest Presidential election since 1916, defeats Republican Thomas E. Dewey, States Rights "Dixiecrat" candidate Strom Thurmond, and Progressive Party candidate Henry A. Wallace
Nov. 7	Returning to Washington, D.C., the Trumans learn they cannot return to White House because it is unsafe structurally. They **move into Blair House** to live until spring 1952 after White House interior has been completely rebuilt

1949

Jan. 5	President first uses term **"Fair Deal"** in message to Congress
April 4	The North Atlantic Treaty (creating **N.A.T.O.**) signed in Washington by U.S. and 11 other nations
June 24	President sends to Congress his **Point Four** plan for assistance to economically underdeveloped areas; enacted June 5, 1950
Sept. 23	President announces that **U.S.S.R.** had exploded an atomic bomb
Oct. 14	Eleven leaders of **U.S. Communist Party** convicted of advocating violent overthrow of U.S. Govt.
Dec. 7	**Nationalist Chinese** government of Chiang Kai-shek flees mainland China (leaving it to the Communists) for the island of Formosa (Taiwan)

1950

Jan. 25	**Alger Hiss**, former State Dept. official, found guilty of perjury for having denied he passed secret documents to Communist spies
Jan. 31	President instructs Atomic Energy Commission to **proceed with hydrogen bomb**
June 25	**North Korea invades** Republic of Korea (June 24, U.S. time)
June 27	President orders Gen. Douglas MacArthur to aid in defense of Republic of Korea, describing it as a **"police action"** to support U.N., whose cease-fire orders had been ignored by North Korea
July 8	**Gen. MacArthur appointed** Commanding General of U.N. Forces in Korea
July 20	Charges made by **Sen. Joseph McCarthy** of large-scale Communist infiltration into State Dept. found to be untrue by a Senate committee
Aug. 27	President orders **seizure by army of all railroads** to prevent general strike
Sept. 22	President **vetoes McCarran Internal Security Act** because it would be ineffective against Communism and strike at "our own liberties"; Congress overrides veto next day
Oct. 15	President **meets with Gen. MacArthur** at Wake Island to discuss differences between them concerning U.S. policy in Eastern Asia
Nov. 1	Two **Puerto Rican nationalists** attempt to shoot their way into Blair House in order to kill President. Guards kill one, wound the other; one guard killed
Dec. 5	**Press Secretary Charley Ross**, an old friend, dies of a heart attack during press briefing

Dec. 16	President declares **national state of emergency** because of Korean conflict

1951

Feb. 28	Preliminary report of **Senate Crime Committee** issued by its chairman, Sen. Estes Kefauver
March 29	Julius and Ethel **Rosenberg found guilty** of conspiracy to commit wartime sabotage (transmitting atomic secrets to Russia), sentenced to death. (Executed in 1953)
April 11	Gen. Douglas **MacArthur relieved** of his Far Eastern Command by President
July 10	Negotiations for **Korean War truce** begin along 38th parallel
Sept. 4	Transcontinental **television** inaugurated with address by President at Japanese Peace Treaty Conference in San Francisco

1952

March 29	President announces he **will not seek reelection**
April 8	President orders **seizure of nation's steel mills** to prevent strike; seizure ruled illegal by U.S. Supreme Court on June 2
May 2	**First jetliner** passenger service begun between London and Johannesburg, South Africa
June 14	President initials keel in plate in dedication of U.S.S. Nautilus, world's first **nuclear-powered submarine**
June 16	**European Coal and Steel Community** Treaty ratified by six Western European nations (forerunner of European Common Market)
July 24	President **commutes death sentence** to life imprisonment of Puerto Rican nationalist who tried to assassinate him
July 25	Gov. **Adlai Stevenson** of Illinois nominated for Presidency by Democrats with President's blessing
July 26	**King Farouk of Egypt** abdicates one week after military coup there
Nov. 1	First **hydrogen device exploded** by U.S. on Eniwetok Island in Pacific; not officially confirmed until 1954
Nov. 4	Gen. **Dwight D. Eisenhower**, a Republican, defeats Democrat Adlai E. Stevenson for Presidency

1953

Jan. 20	President **Eisenhower inaugurated**; President and Mrs. Truman return to home in Independence, Mo.

1955–1956
Publishes **memoirs** in two volumes

1957

Sept. 16	**Truman Library** dedicated in Independence

1965

July 30	President Lyndon B. Johnson flies to Independence to sign **Medicare** (medical care for aged) bill into law at Truman Library in a ceremony honoring Truman

1972

Dec. 26	**Dies** at age 88 in Kansas City hospital

The Truman Library contains much Truman memorabilia, including the round table on which the U.N. Charter was signed in 1945.

Retired but still active around his
home town, Truman was content in his later years to
become simply a "citizen from Independence."